GCSE English

Much Ado About Nothing

by William Shakespeare

Much Ado About Nothing is a brilliant play, but it's not always easy to understand what's going on. Unless you have this CGP book, of course...

It contains the full text of all five acts — and we've explained all the difficult parts in straightforward, day-to-day English. On top of that, we've added helpful notes about the characters, themes, historical background and more.

We've even included plenty of practice questions to test you on what you've learned. You could say we've covered every trick in the book.

D1404603

The Complete Play

CONTENTS

Act One

Act Two

Act Three

Contents

Published by CGP

Editors:
Sophie Herring
Matt Topping

With thanks to Louise McEvoy and Elisabeth Quincey for the proofreading.
With thanks to Ana Pungartnik for the copyright research.

Acknowledgements:

With thanks to Alamy for permission to use the images on pages 1, 4, 5, 6, 26, 50 & 69.

With thanks to Alastair Muir for permission to use the images on pages 3, 6, 7, 38 & 45.

With thanks to ArenaPAL for permission to use the images on pages 5 & 6.

With thanks to Getty Images for permission to use the image on page 2.

With thanks to iStock.com for permission to use the image on page 2.

With thanks to Photostage for permission to use the images on pages 6, 14, 18, 37, 41, 59 & 71.

With thanks to Rex Features for permission to use the images on pages 1, 5, 6, 15, 16, 35, 68 & 75.

With thanks to the Royal Shakespeare Company for permission to use the images on pages 6, 27, 57 & 61.

ISBN: 978 1 78294 852 0
Printed by Elanders Ltd, Newcastle upon Tyne.
Clipart from Corel®

Based on the classic CGP style created by Richard Parsons.

Text, design, layout and original illustrations © Coordination Group Publications Ltd. (CGP) 2018
All rights reserved.

Photocopying more than one chapter of this book is not permitted. Extra copies are available from CGP.
0800 1712 712 • www.cgpbooks.co.uk

Introduction to 'Much Ado About Nothing'

'Much Ado About Nothing' was written by William Shakespeare

- William Shakespeare was an English playwright.

- He wrote some of the most famous plays in the English language, including comedies (such as *Twelfth Night*), tragedies (such as *Romeo and Juliet* and *Hamlet*) and histories (such as *Richard III*).

- *Much Ado About Nothing* is one of Shakespeare's most popular comedies. It was written between 1598 and 1599, and it was first published in 1600.

- The play is about two couples who fall in love in different ways:

© Alastair Muir / REX / Shutterstock

  - Claudio quickly falls in love with Hero, while Benedick and Beatrice argue and insult each other.

  - Benedick and Beatrice say they are opposed to marriage, but they are tricked into falling in love by their friends.

  - Claudio is tricked into believing that Hero has been unfaithful. At their wedding, he refuses to marry her.

  - Hero pretends to be dead until she's proved innocent. The play ends with both couples about to get married.

It's a play with a mix of elements

Shakespeare took the Claudio and Hero love story from earlier European romances, while the Benedick and Beatrice plot was probably his own invention. He uses the two plots to explore contrasting approaches to love and to create tragic scenes as well as comic ones.

© Geraint Lewis / Alamy Stock Photo

- **Love** —
  Claudio falls in love with Hero straightaway, while Benedick and Beatrice grow closer over the course of the play. Both couples face obstacles but ultimately end up together and the play ends happily.

- **Humour** —
  There are lots of comical tricks and misunderstandings, and the language is full of jokes and puns. Some characters are only in the play to make the audience laugh.

- **Tragedy** —
  Even though the play is a comedy, some scenes are dark and serious. Don John's scheming causes tension and leads to the shaming of Hero.

- **Reputation** —
  Honour is important to most of the characters. They want to protect their reputations, which means following society's strict expectations about how they should behave.

Shakespeare's Theatre

Theatre was popular in Shakespeare's time

- Shakespeare was the <u>most successful</u> playwright of his era, but there was plenty of <u>demand</u> for new plays from other playwrights such as <u>Christopher Marlowe</u> and <u>Thomas Kyd</u>.

- The first successful theatres in London were built in the <u>1570s</u>. Plays attracted <u>large crowds</u>, including the most <u>wealthy</u> in society.

- The theatre wasn't just for rich people — Shakespeare's audiences included <u>servants</u> and <u>labourers</u>. The poorer people in the audience stood in <u>front</u> of the stage — if it rained, they got wet.

- There was <u>no electricity</u>, so most plays were put on <u>during the day</u>.

- There wasn't much <u>scenery</u>, and <u>sets</u> were <u>basic</u> so they could be <u>adapted easily</u> to show several different plays.

William Shakespeare

© iStock.com/claudiodivizia

Shakespeare staged his plays at the Globe Theatre

Shakespeare's theatre company performed at the <u>Globe Theatre</u> in London. This is what it might have <u>looked like</u>:

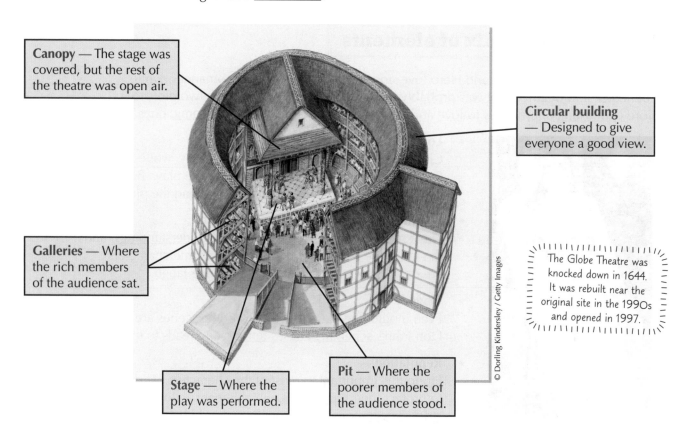

Canopy — The stage was covered, but the rest of the theatre was open air.

Circular building — Designed to give everyone a good view.

Galleries — Where the rich members of the audience sat.

Stage — Where the play was performed.

Pit — Where the poorer members of the audience stood.

The Globe Theatre was knocked down in 1644. It was rebuilt near the original site in the 1990s and opened in 1997.

© Dorling Kindersley / Getty Images

Introduction

Stagecraft

There's more to the play than just the words

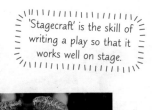

'Stagecraft' is the skill of writing a play so that it works well on stage.

Much Ado About Nothing is meant to be <u>watched</u> not <u>read</u> — when you read the play, <u>imagine</u> how the action would <u>look</u> on stage. You could think about:

Stage directions

- In Act 2, Scene 1, the stage directions say that <u>music</u> should be played — this helps create the <u>lively</u> and <u>light-hearted atmosphere</u> of the <u>masked ball</u>.

Props

- <u>Props</u> would have helped an Elizabethan audience know <u>what was going on</u>. In Act 5, Scene 3, actors are carrying <u>torches</u>, which shows that it's <u>night</u>.

Photograph by Alastair Muir

The horned masks in this production link with the cuckold imagery in the play (see p.13).

Costumes

- Most of the characters are <u>nobles</u> and so in the 1600s they would have worn costumes that suited their <u>high status</u>. Many <u>modern</u> productions continue to dress the characters in <u>extravagant costumes</u>.
- Benedick and Beatrice could be dressed in <u>similar colours</u> to show how <u>alike</u> they are, while Beatrice and Hero could wear very <u>different colours</u> to show the <u>contrast</u> between their characters.

Setting

- The play is set in <u>Messina</u>, a city in Sicily (Italy). This would have seemed <u>exotic</u> to Shakespeare's audience and it is presented as <u>idyllic</u> and <u>peaceful</u>.
- There aren't many different <u>settings</u> within the play — it mostly takes place in Leonato's <u>house</u> and <u>garden</u>, which would be created using <u>scenery</u> and <u>props</u>.

Stage directions tell the actors what to do

When you're reading the play, look at the <u>stage directions</u> — they're little phrases in *italics* that tell the actors <u>what</u> to do, <u>when</u> to come in and when to <u>leave</u> the stage.

These are the really <u>common</u> stage directions in <u>Shakespeare</u>:

Enter	=	when someone <u>comes onto</u> the stage
Exit	=	when one person <u>leaves</u> the stage
Exeunt	=	when <u>more</u> than one person <u>leaves</u> the stage
Aside	=	when a character <u>talks</u> to <u>themselves</u>, the <u>audience</u> or a <u>particular</u> character, but <u>not all</u> characters on stage can <u>hear</u>

Performances of 'Much Ado About Nothing'

'Much Ado About Nothing' was created for a Shakespearean stage

A 2012 production of the play in the rebuilt Globe Theatre.

- In Shakespeare's time only men were allowed to act on stage — female roles were usually played by boys.

- Most of the actors would have worn elaborate costumes based on the fashions of the time.

- Musicians helped to create the atmosphere of a scene, such as at Hero's tomb in Act 5, Scene 3 and at the end of the play to celebrate the double wedding.

The play has been popular for centuries

The way *Much Ado About Nothing* has been performed on stage has changed since Shakespeare's time:

- Women were allowed to perform on stage from 1660. Since then, Beatrice and the other female characters have been played by women.

- In the 1800s, sets, costumes and props became more extravagant. Interpretations of some characters began to change — Beatrice had often been portrayed as bitter, but there was a move towards playing her as warmer and more sympathetic.

- Today, the play is performed in a variety of different ways. In 2012, Iqbal Khan directed a performance with the Royal Shakespeare Company that set the play in Delhi. It explored society's expectations about marriage in present-day India.

There have been lots of adaptations

Much Ado About Nothing has been adapted for film and television, and it has even been made into operas and musicals.

Benedick and Beatrice in Whedon's adaptation.

- Kenneth Branagh's version (1993) was filmed in a villa in Italy to recreate the idyllic setting of Messina. The costumes are quite simple to reflect the relaxed and peaceful atmosphere.

- In David Nicholls' BBC adaptation (2005) of the play, the characters work in a TV studio. Don John is presented as a jealous lover — he wants to break up Claudio and Hero because he loves her but she rejected him.

- Joss Whedon's black and white film (2012) is set in present-day America. It shows Benedick and Beatrice in bed together at the start of the film, but Benedick regrets spending the night with her and leaves — this is used to explain their hostility.

Introduction

Themes and Techniques

'Much Ado About Nothing' is a comedy

- <u>Form</u> — the play has lots of the <u>common features</u> of Shakespeare's <u>comedies</u>, such as <u>young lovers</u> trying to get <u>married</u>, characters wearing <u>disguises</u> and a <u>happy ending</u>.

- <u>Structure</u> — the play has <u>five acts</u>. Acts 1, 2 and 3 <u>lead to</u> the <u>climax</u> in Act 4 when Hero is rejected at the wedding. Everything is then <u>resolved</u> in Act 5.

- <u>Dramatic Irony</u> — this is when the <u>audience</u> knows something the <u>characters don't</u>. It creates <u>humour</u> (Benedick and Beatrice being <u>tricked</u>) but it can also cause <u>tension</u> (Claudio being <u>deceived</u> by Don John).

The themes are the main ideas of the play

When you write about *Much Ado About Nothing*, you'll often have to <u>comment</u> on its <u>themes</u>:

© Nigel Norrington / ArenaPAL

- <u>Love and Marriage</u> — Benedick & Beatrice and Claudio & Hero have <u>contrasting approaches</u> to love and <u>fall in love</u> in different ways.

- <u>Honour and Reputation</u> — The <u>male</u> characters want to <u>protect</u> their <u>reputations</u>. Hero's reputation is <u>ruined</u> and then <u>restored</u>.

- <u>Deception and Misunderstanding</u> — <u>Playful tricks</u> bring the couples together, while Don John <u>deceives</u> other characters to cause <u>conflict</u>.

- <u>Gender</u> — Hero is <u>controlled</u> by the <u>men</u> in the play and characters <u>criticise</u> Beatrice for being an <u>unconventional</u>, <u>independent</u> woman.

The play's language is important

Look out for these <u>techniques</u> as you read the play:

© AF archive / Alamy Stock Photo

- <u>Imagery</u> — <u>metaphors</u> and <u>similes</u> make the language rich and interesting. The <u>tricks</u> are described using <u>hunting</u> imagery to show how Benedick and Beatrice fall into <u>traps</u>.

- <u>Puns and Wordplay</u> — language is used to create <u>humour</u>. Puns are <u>jokes</u> made by <u>twisting</u> the <u>different meanings</u> of a word or playing on two words that <u>sound alike</u>.

- <u>Soliloquies</u> — when <u>characters</u> speak to <u>themselves</u>, revealing their <u>thoughts</u> to the audience. Benedick and Beatrice each have a soliloquy after being <u>tricked</u>, and reveal their <u>changing feelings</u> about <u>marriage</u>.

- <u>Poetry and Prose</u> — most of the play is written in <u>prose</u>, but sometimes characters speak in <u>verse</u>, such as when Claudio <u>accuses</u> Hero at the <u>wedding</u> (see p.37 for more on prose and verse).

Some Cupid kills with arrows, some with traps...

Now that you know about *Much Ado About Nothing's* background, it's time to tackle the play itself. Think about the characters, themes and Shakespeare's techniques as you read through the play — and think about stagecraft too...

© Sam Goldwyn / Renaissance / BBC / Kobal / REX / Shutterstock

Characters

Don Pedro and his men stay with Leonato in Messina

Residents of Messina

Leonato is the governor of Messina.

Photograph by Alastair Muir

© Sam Goldwyn / Renaissance / BBC / Kobal / REX / Shutterstock

Hero is Leonato's daughter.

© Donald Cooper / photostage

Antonio is Leonato's brother.

© Donald Cooper / photostage

Dogberry is the head of the Watch in Messina.

© Donald Cooper / photostage

Margaret and *Ursula* are Hero's serving women.

© Pete Jones / ArenaPAL

Beatrice is Hero's cousin.

Leonato's guests

Don Pedro is the Prince of Aragon.

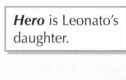

© Photo 12 / Alamy Stock Photo

Photograph by Alastair Muir

Don John is Don Pedro's illegitimate brother.

© Donald Cooper / photostage

Claudio is a friend of Don Pedro.

© AF archive / Alamy Stock Photo

Benedick is a friend of Don Pedro.

Photo by Reg Wilson © RSC.

Borachio and *Conrade* are Don John's followers.

Introduction

Act 1, Scene 1 — Claudio Falls in Love

A messenger tells <u>Leonato</u> that <u>Don Pedro</u> has <u>won</u> the war against his brother <u>Don John</u>. When the soldiers arrive at Leonato's house, <u>Beatrice</u> has fun <u>teasing Benedick</u> and <u>Claudio</u> falls in <u>love</u> with <u>Hero</u>.

Photograph by Alastair Muir

ACT 1, SCENE 1

BEFORE LEONATO'S HOUSE

Enter LEONATO, HERO *and* BEATRICE,
with a MESSENGER

LEONATO	I learn in this letter that Don Pedro of Aragon comes this night to Messina.	
MESSENGER	He is very near by this. He was not three leagues off when I left him.	
LEONATO	How many gentlemen have you lost in this action?	5
MESSENGER	But few of any sort, and none of name.	
LEONATO	A victory is twice itself when the achiever brings home full numbers. I find here that Don Pedro hath bestowed much honour on a young Florentine called Claudio.	10
MESSENGER	Much deserved on his part and equally remembered by Don Pedro. He hath borne himself beyond the promise of his age, doing, in the figure of a lamb, the feats of a lion. He hath indeed better bettered expectation than you must expect of me to tell you how.	15
LEONATO	He hath an uncle here in Messina will be very much glad of it.	
MESSENGER	I have already delivered him letters, and there appears much joy in him — even so much that joy could not show itself modest enough without a badge of bitterness.	20
LEONATO	Did he break out into tears?	
MESSENGER	In great measure.	
LEONATO	A kind overflow of kindness. There are no faces truer than those that are so washed. How much better is it to weep at joy than to joy at weeping!	25
BEATRICE	I pray you, is Signior Mountanto returned from the wars or no?	
MESSENGER	I know none of that name, lady. There was none such in the army of any sort.	30
LEONATO	What is he that you ask for, niece?	
HERO	My cousin means Signior Benedick of Padua.	
MESSENGER	O, he's returned, and as pleasant as ever he was.	
BEATRICE	He set up his bills here in Messina and challenged Cupid at the flight, and my uncle's fool, reading the challenge, subscribed for Cupid, and challenged him at the bird-bolt. I pray you,	35

3 A 'league' is three miles.

6 'Only a few important people and nobody famous.'

Theme — Honour and Reputation

The importance of <u>honour</u> is introduced early on — it's a <u>major theme</u> in the play.

10 A 'Florentine' is a person from Florence.

12-13 'He did far better than you'd expect for his age'.

Character — Claudio

Claudio <u>fought bravely</u> in the war and earned the <u>respect</u> of important men like Don Pedro.

15 'better bettered expectation' means 'done better than expected'.

20-22 'he was so happy that to stop himself from looking big-headed he had to put on a show of sadness.'

28 A 'mountanto' is a fencing move — it means 'upward thrust'. She is sarcastically calling Benedick a 'fancy fighter'.

35-38 'He once put up posters in Messina and challenged Cupid to an archery competition. My uncle's jester competed instead of Cupid and used blunt arrows.' Beatrice is saying that Benedick thinks he's better than Cupid — she thinks he's arrogant and foolish.

Act 1, Scene 1

42-43 'you're too hard on Benedick, but I'm sure he'll match you.'

45 'musty victual' means 'stale food'.

46 'he's an enthusiastic eater'.

47 This means 'appetite for bravery', but Beatrice uses it to mean 'good appetite' — she's mocking Benedick.

Character — Beatrice

Beatrice is confident and witty — she enjoys teasing the messenger and uses lots of wordplay. This contrasts with Hero, who is on stage here but keeps quiet.

57 'skirmish' means 'battle'.

59-65 'He never wins. Last time we argued he ended up totally confused.'

Shakespeare's Techniques

Beatrice uses a simile about fashion to show how quickly Benedick's friendships change.

71 The 'block' is the shaped mould hat-makers use to build a hat on.

73 'an' means 'if'.

75 'squarer' means 'brawler'.

80 'pestilence' means 'plague'.

83 'ere' means 'before'.
83 'a'' means 'he'.
84 'hold' means 'remain'.

	how many hath he killed and eaten in these wars? But how many hath he killed? For indeed I promised to eat all of his killing.	40
LEONATO	Faith, niece, you tax Signior Benedick too much, but he'll be meet with you, I doubt it not.	
MESSENGER	He hath done good service, lady, in these wars.	
BEATRICE	You had musty victual, and he hath holp to eat it: he is a very valiant trencherman — he hath an excellent stomach.	45
MESSENGER	And a good soldier too, lady.	
BEATRICE	And a good soldier to a lady — but what is he to a lord?	50
MESSENGER	A lord to a lord, a man to a man; stuffed with all honourable virtues.	
BEATRICE	It is so, indeed, he is no less than a stuffed man, but for the stuffing — well, we are all mortal.	
LEONATO	You must not, sir, mistake my niece. There is a kind of merry war betwixt Signior Benedick and her: they never meet but there's a skirmish of wit between them.	55
BEATRICE	Alas, he gets nothing by that. In our last conflict four of his five wits went halting off, and now is the whole man governed with one, so that if he have wit enough to keep himself warm, let him bear it for a difference between himself and his horse, for it is all the wealth that he hath left, to be known a reasonable creature. Who is his companion now? He hath every month a new sworn brother.	60 / 65
MESSENGER	Is't possible?	
BEATRICE	Very easily possible. He wears his faith but as the fashion of his hat — it ever changes with the next block.	70
MESSENGER	I see, lady, the gentleman is not in your books.	
BEATRICE	No — an he were, I would burn my study. But, I pray you, who is his companion? Is there no young squarer now that will make a voyage with him to the devil?	75
MESSENGER	He is most in the company of the right noble Claudio.	
BEATRICE	O Lord, he will hang upon him like a disease — he is sooner caught than the pestilence, and the taker runs presently mad. God help the noble Claudio! If he have caught the Benedick, it will cost him a thousand pound ere a' be cured.	80
MESSENGER	I will hold friends with you, lady.	
BEATRICE	Do, good friend.	85
LEONATO	You will never run mad, niece.	

Act 1, Scene 1

BEATRICE	No, not till a hot January.
MESSENGER	Don Pedro is approached.

Enter DON PEDRO, DON JOHN, CLAUDIO,
BENEDICK *and* BALTHASAR

DON PEDRO	Good Signior Leonato, are you come to meet your trouble? The fashion of the world is to avoid cost, and you encounter it.	90
LEONATO	Never came trouble to my house in the likeness of your grace, for trouble being gone, comfort should remain; but when you depart from me, sorrow abides and happiness takes his leave.	95
DON PEDRO	You embrace your charge too willingly. I think this is your daughter.	
LEONATO	Her mother hath many times told me so.	
BENEDICK	Were you in doubt, sir, that you asked her?	
LEONATO	Signior Benedick, no, for then were you a child.	100
DON PEDRO	You have it full, Benedick. We may guess by this what you are, being a man. Truly, the lady fathers herself. Be happy, lady, for you are like an honourable father.	
BENEDICK	If Signior Leonato be her father, she would not have his head on her shoulders for all Messina, as like him as she is. *(Don Pedro and Leonato talk aside)*	105
BEATRICE	I wonder that you will still be talking, Signior Benedick. Nobody marks you.	
BENEDICK	What, my dear Lady Disdain — are you yet living?	110
BEATRICE	Is it possible disdain should die while she hath such meet food to feed it as Signior Benedick? Courtesy itself must convert to disdain, if you come in her presence.	
BENEDICK	Then is courtesy a turncoat. But it is certain I am loved of all ladies — only you excepted — and I would I could find in my heart that I had not a hard heart, for, truly, I love none.	115
BEATRICE	A dear happiness to women, they would else have been troubled with a pernicious suitor. I thank God and my cold blood, I am of your humour for that — I had rather hear my dog bark at a crow than a man swear he loves me.	120
BENEDICK	God keep your ladyship still in that mind so some gentleman or other shall scape a predestinate scratched face.	125
BEATRICE	Scratching could not make it worse, an 'twere such a face as yours were.	
BENEDICK	Well, you are a rare parrot-teacher.	
BEATRICE	A bird of my tongue is better than a beast of yours.	130
BENEDICK	I would my horse had the speed of your tongue,	

90-91 'Most people avoid cost but you go looking for it.'

93-95 'because when trouble goes, it should leave comfort behind, but when you leave me sadness stays behind and happiness leaves.'

102-103 'you can tell who her father is because she looks like him.'

105-106 'she wouldn't want to look like him'.

109 'Nobody's listening.'

Theme — Love and Marriage

Benedick and Beatrice are equally matched in wit and intelligence. This suggests they're well-suited and hints at their future relationship.

112 'meet' means 'suitable'.

113-114 'You'd be enough to turn courtesy herself into disdain (scorn).'

115 'turncoat' means 'traitor'.

120 'pernicious' means 'wicked' or 'harmful'.

121-122 'I agree with you about that'.

125 'scape' means 'escape'.

125 'predestinate' means 'predicted beforehand'.

129 'You go on and on, like someone repeating a phrase for a parrot to learn.'

130 'A bird that talks like me is better than a beast like you.'

Act One

Act 1, Scene 1

134 'You always drop out of the argument like this.'

and so good a continuer. But keep your way, i' God's name — I have done.

BEATRICE
she's hurt, crossed line
You always end with a jade's trick. I know you of old. — 135

DON PEDRO
That is the sum of all, Leonato. *(Turning to the others)* Signior Claudio and Signior Benedick, my dear friend Leonato hath invited you all. I tell him we shall stay here at the least a month, and he heartily prays some occasion may detain us longer. I dare swear he is no hypocrite, but prays from his heart. — 140

143 'forsworn' means 'sworn falsely'.

LEONATO
If you swear, my lord, you shall not be forsworn. *(To Don John)* Let me bid you welcome, my lord, being reconciled to the Prince your brother. I owe you all duty. — 145

Character — Leonato

Leonato is polite and welcoming to his guests.

DON JOHN
I thank you. I am not of many words, but I thank you.

LEONATO
Please it your grace lead on?

DON PEDRO
Your hand, Leonato — we will go together. — 150

Exeunt all except BENEDICK and CLAUDIO

Theme — Deception and Misunderstanding

Characters spend a lot of time 'noting' (observing) each other. Noting often leads to misunderstanding things or being deceived.

CLAUDIO
Benedick, didst thou note the daughter of Signior Leonato?

BENEDICK
I noted her not, but I looked on her.

CLAUDIO
Is she not a modest young lady?

157 'after my custom' means 'as I normally do'.

157-158 'someone who dislikes and criticises women'.

BENEDICK
Do you question me, as an honest man should do, for my simple true judgment, or would you have me speak after my custom, as being a professed tyrant to their sex? — 155

CLAUDIO
No, I pray thee speak in sober judgment.

160 'i'faith' means 'honestly'.

162-165 'I'll say this much for her: if she was any different she wouldn't be good-looking, and I don't like her the way she is.'

BENEDICK
Why, i' faith, methinks she's too low for a high praise, too brown for a fair praise and too little for a great praise. Only this commendation I can afford her, that were she other than she is, she were unhandsome, and being no other but as she is, I do not like her. — 160 ... 165

Shakespeare's Techniques

Claudio uses a metaphor to describe how beautiful Hero is, but this also makes her sound like a possession.

CLAUDIO
Thou thinkest I am in sport: I pray thee tell me truly how thou lik'st her.

BENEDICK
Would you buy her, that you inquire after her?

CLAUDIO
Can the world buy such a jewel?

BENEDICK
Yea, and a case to put it into. But speak you this with a sad brow, or do you play the flouting jack, to tell us Cupid is a good hare-finder and Vulcan a rare carpenter? Come, in what key shall a man take you, to go in the song? — 170

171 A 'flouting jack' is someone who says the opposite of what they mean.

172-173 Cupid was known as a bad shot, and Vulcan was a blacksmith, not a carpenter.

173-174 'How am I supposed to interpret what you're saying?'

CLAUDIO
In mine eye she is the sweetest lady that ever I looked on. — 175

BENEDICK
I can see yet without spectacles and I see no

Act 1, Scene 1

	such matter. There's her cousin, an' she were not possessed with a fury, exceeds her as much in beauty as the first of May doth the last of December. But I hope you have no intent to turn husband, have you?	180
CLAUDIO	I would scarce trust myself, though I had sworn the contrary, if Hero would be my wife.	
BENEDICK	Is't come to this? In faith, hath not the world one man but he will wear his cap with suspicion? Shall I never see a bachelor of three-score again? Go to, i' faith, an thou wilt needs thrust thy neck into a yoke, wear the print of it and sigh away Sundays. Look, Don Pedro is returned to seek you.	185
		190
	Enter DON PEDRO	
DON PEDRO	What secret hath held you here, that you followed not to Leonato's?	
BENEDICK	I would your grace would constrain me to tell.	
DON PEDRO	I charge thee on thy allegiance.	195
BENEDICK	You hear, Count Claudio. I can be secret as a dumb man. I would have you think so — but, on my allegiance, mark you this, on my allegiance — he is in love. With who? Now that is your grace's part. Mark how short his answer is — with Hero, Leonato's short daughter.	200
CLAUDIO	If this were so, so were it uttered.	
BENEDICK	Like the old tale, my lord: 'it is not so, nor 'twas not so, but, indeed, God forbid it should be so.'	
CLAUDIO	If my passion change not shortly, God forbid it should be otherwise.	205
DON PEDRO	Amen, if you love her, for the lady is very well worthy.	
CLAUDIO	You speak this to fetch me in, my lord.	
DON PEDRO	By my troth, I speak my thought.	210
CLAUDIO	And, in faith, my lord, I spoke mine.	
BENEDICK	And, by my two faiths and troths, my lord, I spoke mine.	
CLAUDIO	That I love her, I feel.	
DON PEDRO	That she is worthy, I know.	215
BENEDICK	That I neither feel how she should be loved nor know how she should be worthy, is the opinion that fire cannot melt out of me — I will die in it at the stake.	
DON PEDRO	Thou wast ever an obstinate heretic in the despite of beauty.	220
CLAUDIO	And never could maintain his part but in the force of his will.	

Context — Cuckolds

This is a reference to cuckolds (see p.13) — men might wear caps to hide horns on their heads. The reference shows Benedick's disbelief that Claudio wants to get married.

187 'three-score' is 'sixty'.

188-190 'Go ahead then, if you want to get married and give up all your fun and freedom.'

194 'I wish you would force me to tell you.'

195 'I order you to tell me.'

202 'If it's true, that's what he would say.'

209 'You're just saying that to get me to give myself away'.

210 'By my troth' means 'I swear'.

212 'on my word of honour to you both'.

Shakespeare's Techniques

Don Pedro uses repetition to show support to Claudio. Benedick uses it to mock the other two.

220-221 'You've always refused to acknowledge beauty.'

222-223 'He only keeps the pretence up by willpower.'

Act 1, Scene 1

226-228 Benedick's saying he won't have anything to do with women because he doesn't want to be made a fool of if his wife sleeps with other men.

230 'fine' means 'result'.

235-239 'if I do ever fall in love, feel free to mock me.'

240-241 'Well, if you ever change your mind, you'll be a popular topic of conversation.'

242 A 'bottle' is a 'basket' used for archery practice.

244 There was a famous archer called Adam Bell.

245 'time will be the test of that'.

245-246 An old saying, meaning 'everyone can be tamed eventually'.

Shakespeare's Techniques

Benedick's use of cuckold imagery (see p.13) and clever language shows he is witty, but it also shows his strong mistrust of women.

255-256 'If Cupid hasn't used up all his arrows in Venice, you'll suffer for this soon enough.'

258 'Well, you'll soften up in time.'

259-260 'go into Leonato's house.'

263-264 'I think I can do the job'.

264-266 These are all traditional letter endings, like 'yours sincerely'.

267-269 'The stuff you say is often pretty silly too.'

BENEDICK	That a woman conceived me, I thank her; that she brought me up, I likewise give her most humble thanks: but that I will have a recheat winded in my forehead, or hang my bugle in an invisible baldrick, all women shall pardon me. Because I will not do them the wrong to mistrust any, I will do myself the right to trust none: and the fine is, for the which I may go the finer, I will live a bachelor.	225 / 230
DON PEDRO	I shall see thee, ere I die, look pale with love.	
BENEDICK	With anger, with sickness, or with hunger, my lord, not with love: prove that ever I lose more blood with love than I will get again with drinking, pick out mine eyes with a ballad-maker's pen and hang me up at the door of a brothel-house for the sign of blind Cupid.	235
DON PEDRO	Well, if ever thou dost fall from this faith, thou wilt prove a notable argument.	240
BENEDICK	If I do, hang me in a bottle like a cat and shoot at me, and he that hits me, let him be clapped on the shoulder, and called Adam.	
DON PEDRO	Well, as time shall try — 'In time the savage bull doth bear the yoke.'	245
BENEDICK	The savage bull may — but if ever the sensible Benedick bear it, pluck off the bull's horns and set them in my forehead, and let me be vilely painted, and in such great letters as they write 'Here is good horse to hire' let them signify under my sign 'Here you may see Benedick the married man.'	250
CLAUDIO	If this should ever happen, thou wouldst be horn-mad.	
DON PEDRO	Nay, if Cupid have not spent all his quiver in Venice, thou wilt quake for this shortly.	255
BENEDICK	I look for an earthquake too, then.	
DON PEDRO	Well, you will temporize with the hours. In the meantime, good Signior Benedick, repair to Leonato's. Commend me to him and tell him I will not fail him at supper; for indeed he hath made great preparation.	260
BENEDICK	I have almost matter enough in me for such an embassage, and so I commit you —	
CLAUDIO	To the tuition of God. From my house, if I had it —	265
DON PEDRO	The sixth of July. Your loving friend, Benedick.	
BENEDICK	Nay, mock not, mock not. The body of your discourse is sometime guarded with fragments, and the guards are but slightly basted on neither. Ere you flout old ends any further, examine your conscience — and so I leave you.	270

Exit

Act 1, Scene 1

CLAUDIO	My liege, your highness now may do me good.
DON PEDRO	My love is thine to teach. Teach it but how,
	And thou shalt see how apt it is to learn
	Any hard lesson that may do thee good. 275
CLAUDIO	Hath Leonato any son, my lord?
DON PEDRO	No child but Hero, she's his only heir.
	Dost thou affect her, Claudio?
CLAUDIO	O, my lord,
	When you went onward on this ended action,
	I looked upon her with a soldier's eye, 280
	That liked, but had a rougher task in hand
	Than to drive liking to the name of love;
	But now I am returned and that war-thoughts
	Have left their places vacant, in their rooms
	Come thronging soft and delicate desires, 285
	All prompting me how fair young Hero is,
	Saying, I liked her ere I went to wars.
DON PEDRO	Thou wilt be like a lover presently
	And tire the hearer with a book of words.
	If thou dost love fair Hero, cherish it, 290
	And I will break with her and with her father,
	And thou shalt have her. Was't not to this end
	That thou began'st to twist so fine a story?
CLAUDIO	How sweetly you do minister to love,
	That know love's grief by his complexion! 295
	But lest my liking might too sudden seem,
	I would have salved it with a longer treatise.
DON PEDRO	What need the bridge much broader
	than the flood?
	The fairest grant is the necessity.
	Look, what will serve is fit: 'tis once, thou lovest, 300
	And I will fit thee with the remedy.
	I know we shall have revelling to-night.
	I will assume thy part in some disguise
	And tell fair Hero I am Claudio,
	And in her bosom I'll unclasp my heart 305
	And take her hearing prisoner with the force
	And strong encounter of my amorous tale.
	Then after to her father will I break,
	And the conclusion is, she shall be thine.
	In practice let us put it presently. 310

Exeunt

Shakespeare's Techniques

Claudio and Don Pedro start speaking in blank verse (see p.37) when they discuss the plan to woo Hero. This makes them sound romantic and noble.

273-275 'Just tell me how I can help you.'

278 'affect' means 'love'.

279 'this ended action' means 'the war that's just finished'.

Theme — Love and Marriage

Claudio contrasts being a soldier with falling in love. This shows the different sides to his character.

291 'I will speak to her and her father'.

294-295 'You certainly know love when you see it!'

297 'I would have given a longer explanation of my feelings.'

298-300 'Why speak for longer than you need to? Just do what you need to do. You love her — that's all I need to know'.

302 'revelling' means 'a party'.

Character — Don Pedro

Don Pedro is a loyal friend — he thinks up a plan to help Claudio woo Hero.

305-307 'I'll confess my feelings for her and win her with my love story.'

Context — Cuckolds

The Elizabethans joked that men with unfaithful wives became cuckolds who grew horns on their foreheads. Men were seen as weak if their wives cheated on them, so they were afraid of this happening. There are lots of references to horns and cuckolds in the play which create humour and emphasise that the male characters are distrustful of women.

Act One

Act 1, Scene 2 — Antonio Tells Leonato a Rumour

© Donald Cooper / photostage

Antonio tells Leonato he's heard a <u>rumour</u> that <u>Don Pedro</u> loves <u>Hero</u> and wants to <u>marry</u> her. Leonato is happy for his daughter to marry a <u>respected man</u> and tells Antonio to go and give Hero the good news.

Character — Antonio

Antonio is <u>loyal</u> to his <u>brother</u> — he tells him the news to <u>help</u> him. But he looks <u>foolish</u> to the audience as his information <u>isn't true</u>.

6-7 'We'll see how things turn out in the end, but they look good on the surface.'

8 A 'thick-pleached alley' is a path shaded by branches.

10 'discovered' means 'admitted'.

13 'accordant' means 'agreeing'.

13-14 'he would act on the spur of the moment and tell you all about it immediately.'

18-19 'We'll just treat it like a dream until it actually happens, but I'll let my daughter know'.

21 'peradventure' means 'perhaps'.

Theme — Gender

As her <u>father</u>, Leonato <u>decides</u> who Hero will <u>marry</u> — she <u>doesn't</u> get a <u>choice</u> in the matter.

ACT 1, SCENE 2

A ROOM IN LEONATO'S HOUSE

Enter LEONATO *and* ANTONIO, *meeting*

LEONATO How now, brother! Where is my cousin, your son? Hath he provided this music?

ANTONIO He is very busy about it. But, brother, I can tell you strange news that you yet dreamt not of.

LEONATO Are they good? 5

ANTONIO As the event stamps them, but they have a good cover; they show well outward. The Prince and Count Claudio, walking in a thick-pleached alley in mine orchard, were thus much overheard by a man of mine — the prince discovered to Claudio 10 that he loved my niece your daughter and meant to acknowledge it this night in a dance, and if he found her accordant, he meant to take the present time by the top and instantly break with you of it.

LEONATO Hath the fellow any wit that told you this? 15

ANTONIO A good sharp fellow — I will send for him, and question him yourself.

LEONATO No, no. We will hold it as a dream till it appear itself, but I will acquaint my daughter withal, that she may be the better prepared for an answer, if 20 peradventure this be true. Go you and tell her of it.

Enter Antonio's son with a musician and attendants

Cousins, you know what you have to do. *(To musician)* O, I cry you mercy, friend, go you with me, and I will use your skill. Good cousin, have a care this busy time. 25

Exeunt

Theme — Deception and Misunderstanding

Antonio <u>mistakenly</u> thinks that Don Pedro wants to marry Hero — his servant <u>overheard</u> Don Pedro's plan to help Claudio and <u>misunderstood</u>. Lots of the <u>tricks</u> and <u>deceptions</u> in the play happen because characters <u>observe</u> each other or <u>overhear</u> things and they <u>misunderstand</u> what's going on.

Act 1, Scene 3 — Don John Plans to Cause Trouble

Don John is <u>miserable</u> and feels <u>resentful</u> towards his <u>brother</u>. Borachio tells him he's heard Claudio wants to <u>marry Hero</u>, so Don John decides to try to <u>ruin</u> their relationship.

© Sam Goldwyn / Renaissance / BBC / Kobal / REX / Shutterstock

ACT 1, SCENE 3

A ROOM IN LEONATO'S HOUSE

Enter DON JOHN *and* CONRADE

CONRADE	What the goodyear, my lord? Why are you thus out of measure sad?	
DON JOHN	There is no measure in the occasion that breeds, therefore the sadness is without limit.	
CONRADE	You should hear reason.	5
DON JOHN	And when I have heard it, what blessing brings it?	
CONRADE	If not a present remedy, at least a patient sufferance.	
DON JOHN	I wonder that thou, being, as thou sayest thou art, born under Saturn, goest about to apply a moral medicine to a mortifying mischief. I cannot hide what I am — I must be sad when I have cause and smile at no man's jests, eat when I have stomach and wait for no man's leisure, sleep when I am drowsy and tend on no man's business, laugh when I am merry and claw no man in his humour.	10 15
CONRADE	Yea, but you must not make the full show of this till you may do it without controlment. You have of late stood out against your brother, and he hath ta'en you newly into his grace, where it is impossible you should take true root but by the fair weather that you make yourself — it is needful that you frame the season for your own harvest.	20
DON JOHN	I had rather be a canker in a hedge than a rose in his grace, and it better fits my blood to be disdained of all than to fashion a carriage to rob love from any. In this, though I cannot be said to be a flattering honest man, it must not be denied but I am a plain-dealing villain. I am trusted with a muzzle and enfranchised with a clog; therefore I have decreed not to sing in my cage. If I had my mouth, I would bite; if I had my liberty, I would do my liking. In the meantime let me be that I am and seek not to alter me.	25 30 35
CONRADE	Can you make no use of your discontent?	
DON JOHN	I make all use of it, for I use it only. Who comes here?	

Enter BORACHIO

What news, Borachio?

Margin notes:

1-2 'What's wrong, my lord? Why are you so sad?'

3 'There's no good reason for me to be sad'.

7-8 'If it won't make you happier, at least it will make your sadness easier to put up with.'

9-11 'I think it's a bit odd that someone as miserable as you is trying to cheer me up.'

16 'claw' means 'flatter'.

Theme — Loyalty

Don Pedro has <u>forgiven</u> Don John for <u>fighting</u> against him, but Don John still <u>resents</u> his brother.

21-24 'you won't get properly back into his good books unless you act pleasantly. Behave yourself now and you'll reap the benefits later.'

25 A 'canker' is a type of wild rose, but 'canker' can also mean 'rot' or 'disease'.

Character — Don John

Don John knows that people <u>dislike</u> him, but he <u>isn't</u> going to <u>change</u> who he is just to make them <u>like</u> him.

30-31 'I'm not really trusted or properly free'.

Handwritten annotations: "= irritating" (near line 25)

Act One

Act 1, Scene 3

Theme — Love
and Marriage

Like Benedick, Don John
<u>criticises marriage</u>. Many
of the <u>male</u> characters
are <u>suspicious</u> of <u>women</u>.

47 'Marry' means 'why'.

53 'Cheeky little monkey!'

55 'I was doing a perfumer's job'.
A perfumer's job was to scent rooms.

57 'in sad conference' means
'having a serious conversation'.

57-58 'I hid behind a tapestry'.

Theme — Deception
and Misunderstanding

Borachio <u>overheard</u>
Don Pedro's <u>plan</u>, just like
Antonio says his servant
did — except Borachio
<u>understood</u> it <u>correctly</u>.

61 'let us thither'
means 'let's go there'.

62-63 'That youngster has all the
glory that should have been mine'.

69 'Shall we go and
see what we can do?'

BORACHIO	I came yonder from a great supper. The prince your brother is royally entertained by Leonato, and I can give you intelligence of an intended marriage. *advice/insight*	40
DON JOHN	Will it serve for any model to build mischief on? What is he for a fool that betroths himself to unquietness?	45
BORACHIO	Marry, it is your brother's right hand.	
DON JOHN	Who, the most exquisite Claudio?	
BORACHIO	Even he.	
DON JOHN	A proper squire! And who, and who? Which way looks he?	50
BORACHIO	Marry, on Hero, the daughter and heir of Leonato.	
DON JOHN	A very forward March-chick! How came you to this?	
BORACHIO	Being entertained for a perfumer, as I was smoking a musty room, comes me the prince and Claudio, hand in hand in sad conference. I whipt me behind the arras, and there heard it agreed upon that the prince should woo Hero for himself, and having obtained her, give her to Count Claudio.	55 ... 60
DON JOHN	Come, come, let us thither. This may prove food to my displeasure. That young start-up hath all the glory of my overthrow: if I can cross him any way, I bless myself every way. You are both sure, and will assist me?	65
CONRADE	To the death, my lord.	
DON JOHN	Let us to the great supper — their cheer is the greater that I am subdued. Would the cook were of my mind! Shall we go prove what's to be done?	
BORACHIO	We'll wait upon your lordship.	70
	Exeunt	

Shakespeare's Techniques — Form

This is a <u>comedy</u>, so the audience knows the
play will have a <u>happy ending</u>. They expect
the characters to face <u>challenges</u> along the
way, but ultimately all the <u>problems</u> will be
<u>resolved</u> and the <u>couples</u> will end up <u>together</u>.

This means the audience knows that Don John
<u>won't succeed</u> in the end. He <u>isn't</u> a very
<u>complex villain</u> — his only purpose in the
play is to cause <u>conflict</u> and create <u>obstacles</u>
for the characters to <u>overcome</u>.

© Sam Goldwyn / Renaissance /
BBC / Kobal / REX / Shutterstock

Act One — Practice Questions

Quick Questions

1) Which character earned an honourable reputation in the war?

2) Who does Benedick call "Lady Disdain"?

3) Who invites the other characters to stay at his house?

4) What is Don Pedro going to do at the party that night?

5) Which characters speak in verse in Act 1, Scene 1?

6) What is a cuckold?

7) Who tells Leonato that Don Pedro wants to marry Hero?

8) How did Borachio find out that Claudio wants to marry Hero?

9) Why does Don John dislike Claudio?

In-depth Questions

1) Using Act 1 as a starting point, write down one word for each of the following characters that describes their personality:
   a) Beatrice   b) Benedick   c) Claudio   d) Don Pedro

2) How does Shakespeare present Benedick and Beatrice's relationship in Act 1?

3) Explain Benedick's attitude to marriage in Act 1, Scene 1.

4) Give two examples of how Shakespeare uses language to create humour in Act 1.

5) Why do you think Don Pedro offers to help Claudio woo Hero?

6) Explain how Shakespeare introduces the theme of loyalty in Act 1.

7) Explain how Don John is introduced as the villain of the play in Act 1.

8) Give two examples of imagery from Act 1, Scene 1 and explain each of their effects.

9) Write a diary entry for Claudio explaining how he feels about Hero in Act 1.

Act 2, Scene 1 — Don Pedro Woos Hero

© Donald Cooper / photostage

At the <u>masked ball</u>, Don Pedro <u>woos</u> Hero for Claudio and Beatrice <u>insults</u> Benedick. Don John tries to <u>trick</u> Claudio — he says that Don Pedro wants Hero for himself. Don Pedro explains it's <u>not true</u> and Leonato <u>agrees</u> that Hero can marry Claudio. Don Pedro decides to <u>trick</u> Beatrice and Benedick into <u>falling in love</u>.

ACT 2, SCENE 1

A HALL IN LEONATO'S HOUSE

Enter LEONATO, ANTONIO, HERO, BEATRICE *and others*

LEONATO	Was not Count John here at supper?
ANTONIO	I saw him not.
BEATRICE	How tartly that gentleman looks! I never can see him but I am heart-burned an hour after.
HERO	He is of a very melancholy disposition.
BEATRICE	He were an excellent man that were made just in the midway between him and Benedick. The one is too like an image and says nothing, and the other too like my lady's eldest son, evermore tattling.
LEONATO	Then half Signior Benedick's tongue in Count John's mouth, and half Count John's melancholy in Signior Benedick's face —
BEATRICE	With a good leg and a good foot, uncle, and money enough in his purse — such a man would win any woman in the world, if a' could get her good-will.
LEONATO	By my troth, niece, thou wilt never get thee a husband, if thou be so shrewd of thy tongue.
ANTONIO	In faith, she's too curst.
BEATRICE	Too curst is more than curst. I shall lessen God's sending that way, for it is said, 'God sends a curst cow short horns' but to a cow too curst he sends none.
LEONATO	So, by being too curst, God will send you no horns.
BEATRICE	Just, if he send me no husband, for the which blessing I am at him upon my knees every morning and evening. Lord, I could not endure a husband with a beard on his face — I had rather lie in the woollen.
LEONATO	You may light on a husband that hath no beard.
BEATRICE	What should I do with him? Dress him in my apparel and make him my waiting-gentlewoman? He that hath a beard is more than a youth, and he that hath no beard is less than a man; and he that is more than a youth is not for me, and he that is less than a man, I am not for him. Therefore, I will even take sixpence in earnest of

Line numbers: 5, 10, 15, 20, 25, 30, 35

3 'tartly' means 'bitterly'.

5 'melancholy' means 'miserable'.

9-10 'like a spoilt child, always prattling away.'

16 'a'' means 'he'.

19 'if you make such cutting comments.'

Character — Beatrice

Beatrice <u>doesn't conform</u> to the <u>behaviour</u> the men expect from <u>women</u>, and she <u>ignores</u> their criticism.

20 'curst' means 'grumpy'.

21-24 She's saying that God limits how much harm bad things can do. So a bad-tempered cow would be given short horns so that it couldn't do much harm. A really vicious cow wouldn't be given horns at all.

30 'lie in the woollen' means 'sleep in itchy woollen sheets'.

Theme — Love and Marriage

Beatrice sets <u>impossible</u> standards for a <u>husband</u> to emphasise that she <u>doesn't</u> want one — she <u>refuses</u> to marry a man either <u>with</u> a <u>beard</u> or <u>without</u> one.

Act 2, Scene 1

the bearward, and lead his apes into hell.

LEONATO Well, then, go you into hell? 40

BEATRICE No, but to the gate — and there will the devil meet me, like an old cuckold, with horns on his head, and say 'Get you to heaven, Beatrice, get you to heaven. Here's no place for you maids.' So deliver I up my apes, and away to Saint Peter for 45 the heavens. He shows me where the bachelors sit, and there live we as merry as the day is long.

ANTONIO *(To Hero)* Well, niece, I trust you will be ruled by your father.

BEATRICE Yes, faith. It is my cousin's duty to make curtsy 50 and say 'Father, as it please you.' But yet for all that, cousin, let him be a handsome fellow, or else make another curtsy and say 'Father, as it please me.'

LEONATO Well, niece, I hope to see you one day fitted with 55 a husband.

BEATRICE Not till God make men of some other metal than earth. Would it not grieve a woman to be overmastered with a piece of valiant dust? To make an account of her life to a clod of wayward 60 marl? No, uncle, I'll none. Adam's sons are my brethren, and, truly, I hold it a sin to match in my kindred.

LEONATO Daughter, remember what I told you — if the Prince do solicit you in that kind, you know your 65 answer.

BEATRICE The fault will be in the music, cousin, if you be not wooed in good time. If the Prince be too important, tell him there is measure in every thing and so dance out the answer. For, hear me, 70 Hero — wooing, wedding, and repenting, is as a Scotch jig, a measure, and a cinque pace: the first suit is hot and hasty, like a Scotch jig, and full as fantastical; the wedding, mannerly-modest, as a measure, full of state and anciency; and then 75 comes repentance and, with his bad legs, falls into the cinque pace faster and faster, till he sink into his grave.

LEONATO Cousin, you apprehend passing shrewdly.

BEATRICE I have a good eye, uncle — I can see a church by 80 daylight.

LEONATO The revellers are entering, brother. Make good room.

All put on their masks

Enter DON PEDRO, CLAUDIO, BENEDICK,
BALTHASAR, DON JOHN, BORACHIO,
MARGARET, URSULA *and others, masked*

38-39 A 'bearward' was a bear keeper who might also have kept apes. Leading apes around hell was supposed to be the punishment for unmarried women.

44 'maids' means 'unmarried women' or 'virgins'.

44-46 'So I'll hand over my apes and go up to Saint Peter in heaven.'

Theme — Gender

Leonato and Antonio think it is a woman's <u>duty</u> to <u>obey</u> her <u>father</u>. Beatrice thinks that Hero should be given a <u>choice</u> in who she <u>marries</u>.

60-61 'wayward marl' means 'unruly clay'. In the Bible, God made the first man (Adam) from clay.

61-63 'Adam's sons are my brothers, and I believe it's a sin to marry within the family.'

64-65 'if the Prince (Don Pedro) asks you to marry him'.

68-70 'If the Prince is too hasty, tell him everything comes in its own good time, and delay giving your answer.'

Shakespeare's Techniques

Beatrice uses <u>similes</u> to compare the <u>stages</u> of <u>romance</u> to different <u>dances</u>. She thinks that relationships follow a <u>predictable pattern</u>.

72 a 'Scotch jig' is a fast, energetic dance.

72 a 'measure' is a slow, dignified dance.

72 a 'cinque pace' is a fast, jerky dance.

79 'you are very observant.'

82 'revellers' means 'guests at the masked ball'.

Act 2, Scene 1

Hero speaks more <u>openly</u> and <u>wittily</u> than she has before — <u>social conventions</u> are <u>less strict</u> at the <u>masked ball</u>.

91 'favour' means 'looks'.

91-92 'God forbid your face looks like that mask!'

93-94 In Roman mythology, Philemon was a poor man who invited Jove (the king of the gods) into his run-down cottage for a meal. Don Pedro is saying that his face is better than his mask.

107 'clerk' means 'priest'.

Shakespeare uses the <u>masks</u> to create <u>humour</u> in this scene, but they also <u>emphasise</u> the theme of <u>deception</u> and <u>misunderstanding</u>.

112 'counterfeit' means 'pretend to be'.

113 'You could never do such a bad impression of him'.

118-120 'Go on, quiet now, I know it's you. Good qualities always show through.'

DON PEDRO	Lady, will you walk about with your friend?	
HERO	So you walk softly and look sweetly and say nothing, I am yours for the walk; and especially when I walk away.	85
DON PEDRO	With me in your company?	
HERO	I may say so, when I please.	
DON PEDRO	And when please you to say so?	90
HERO	When I like your favour, for God defend the lute should be like the case!	
DON PEDRO	My visor is Philemon's roof — Within the house is Jove.	
HERO	Why, then, your visor should be thatched.	95
DON PEDRO	Speak low, if you speak love.	

They move aside

BALTHASAR	Well, I would you did like me.	
MARGARET	So would not I, for your own sake, for I have many ill-qualities.	
BALTHASAR	Which is one?	100
MARGARET	I say my prayers aloud.	
BALTHASAR	I love you the better — the hearers may cry 'Amen.'	
MARGARET	God match me with a good dancer!	
BALTHASAR	Amen.	105
MARGARET	And God keep him out of my sight when the dance is done! Answer, clerk.	
BALTHASAR	No more words — the clerk is answered.	

They move aside

URSULA	I know you well enough. You are Signior Antonio.	
ANTONIO	At a word, I am not.	110
URSULA	I know you by the waggling of your head.	
ANTONIO	To tell you true, I counterfeit him.	
URSULA	You could never do him so ill-well, unless you were the very man. Here's his dry hand up and down — you are he, you are he.	115
ANTONIO	At a word, I am not.	
URSULA	Come, come, do you think I do not know you by your excellent wit? Can virtue hide itself? Go to, mum, you are he. Graces will appear, and there's an end.	120

They move aside

BEATRICE	Will you not tell me who told you so?	
BENEDICK	No, you shall pardon me.	
BEATRICE	Nor will you not tell me who you are?	
BENEDICK	Not now.	

Act 2, Scene 1

BEATRICE	That I was disdainful, and that I had my good wit out of the *Hundred Merry Tales* — well, this was Signior Benedick that said so.	125
BENEDICK	What's he?	
BEATRICE	I am sure you know him well enough.	
BENEDICK	Not I, believe me.	130
BEATRICE	Did he never make you laugh?	
BENEDICK	I pray you, what is he?	
BEATRICE	Why, he is the Prince's jester, a very dull fool. Only his gift is in devising impossible slanders. None but libertines delight in him, and the commendation is not in his wit, but in his villainy, for he both pleases men and angers them, and then they laugh at him and beat him. I am sure he is in the fleet. I would he had boarded me.	135
BENEDICK	When I know the gentleman, I'll tell him what you say.	140
BEATRICE	Do, do. He'll but break a comparison or two on me, which, peradventure not marked or not laughed at, strikes him into melancholy, and then there's a partridge wing saved, for the fool will eat no supper that night.	145

Music

	We must follow the leaders.	
BENEDICK	In every good thing.	
BEATRICE	Nay, if they lead to any ill, I will leave them at the next turning.	150

Dance

Then exeunt all except DON JOHN, BORACHIO *and* CLAUDIO

DON JOHN	Sure my brother is amorous on Hero and hath withdrawn her father to break with him about it. The ladies follow her and but one visor remains.	
BORACHIO	And that is Claudio. I know him by his bearing.	
DON JOHN	Are not you Signior Benedick?	155
CLAUDIO	You know me well — I am he.	
DON JOHN	Signior, you are very near my brother in his love; he is enamoured on Hero. I pray you, dissuade him from her; she is no equal for his birth — you may do the part of an honest man in it.	160
CLAUDIO	How know you he loves her?	
DON JOHN	I heard him swear his affection.	
BORACHIO	So did I too, and he swore he would marry her tonight.	
DON JOHN	Come, let us to the banquet.	165

Exeunt DON JOHN *and* BORACHIO

126 The *Hundred Merry Tales* was a book of crude, bad jokes.

Theme — Deception and Misunderstanding

Benedick tries to trick Beatrice, but she sees through his disguise. The women in the play are often less easy to deceive than the men.

134 'His only talent is coming up with ridiculous insults.'

135 'libertines' means 'immoral people'.

138-139 'I'm sure he's in the crowd somewhere. I wish he had come to fight me.'

142-144 'He'll just make a couple of jokes at my expense, and when no one notices or laughs at them, he'll start sulking'.

Shakespeare's Techniques

These comments are ironic and foreshadow the wedding. When Claudio and Don Pedro shame Hero, Benedick and Beatrice see it is wrong and don't follow them.

153 'visor' means 'mask'.

Theme — Deception and Misunderstanding

Don John pretends to think that Claudio is Benedick. He takes advantage of the masked ball to trick Claudio.

Act 2, Scene 1

Character — Claudio

Claudio is <u>jealous</u> and <u>suspicious</u> — he quickly <u>believes</u> Don John's <u>lies</u>, even though Don Pedro is his <u>friend</u>.

171-176 'People in love should speak for themselves, not trust others, because beauty's more powerful than loyalty. I should've known better.'

180 'Whither' means 'where'.

181-182 A garland made of willow branches (worn on the head or around the neck) traditionally symbolised someone who'd been abandoned by their lover.

183 A 'usurer' is a moneylender.

188 A 'drover' is someone who sells cows.

190 'served you thus' means 'treated you like this'.

192-193 'Don't take it out on me! It's nothing to do with me.'

Shakespeare's Techniques

Benedick uses a <u>natural metaphor</u> — he describes Claudio as an <u>injured bird</u> hiding in a <u>bush</u> to show how <u>upset</u> he is.

199-202 'I shouldn't be so hard on myself. That's not my reputation. It's Beatrice's bitterness that makes her talk as though what she thinks about me is what everyone thinks.'

206-207 'Honestly, my lord, I have reported on what's going on.'

207-208 'as miserable as a shed in a warren.' A 'warren' was a place where rabbits were bred for eating. The 'lodge' would be remote with not much else nearby.

CLAUDIO	Thus answer I in the name of Benedick,	
	But hear these ill news with the ears of Claudio.	
	'Tis certain so, the prince woos for himself.	
	Friendship is constant in all other things	
	Save in the office and affairs of love.	170
	Therefore, all hearts in love use their own tongues,	
	Let every eye negotiate for itself	
	And trust no agent, for beauty is a witch	
	Against whose charms faith melteth into blood.	
	This is an accident of hourly proof,	175
	Which I mistrusted not. Farewell, therefore, Hero!	

Re-enter BENEDICK

BENEDICK	Count Claudio?	
CLAUDIO	Yea, the same.	
BENEDICK	Come, will you go with me?	
CLAUDIO	Whither?	180
BENEDICK	Even to the next willow, about your own business, county. What fashion will you wear the garland of? About your neck, like an usurer's chain? Or under your arm, like a lieutenant's scarf? You must wear it one way, for the prince hath got your Hero.	185
CLAUDIO	I wish him joy of her.	
BENEDICK	Why, that's spoken like an honest drover. So they sell bullocks. But did you think the Prince would have served you thus?	190
CLAUDIO	I pray you, leave me.	
BENEDICK	Ho! Now you strike like the blind man! 'Twas the boy that stole your meat, and you'll beat the post.	
CLAUDIO	If it will not be, I'll leave you.	

Exit

BENEDICK	Alas, poor hurt fowl! Now will he creep into sedges. But that my Lady Beatrice should know me, and not know me! The Prince's fool! Ha? It may be I go under that title because I am merry. Yea, but so I am apt to do myself wrong. I am not so reputed. It is the base, though bitter, disposition of Beatrice that puts the world into her person and so gives me out. Well, I'll be revenged as I may.	195 200

Re-enter DON PEDRO

DON PEDRO	Now, signior, where's the count? Did you see him?	205
BENEDICK	Troth, my lord, I have played the part of Lady Fame. I found him here as melancholy as a lodge in a warren. I told him, and I think I told him true, that your grace had got the good will of this young lady, and I offered him my company	210

Act 2, Scene 1

to a willow-tree, either to make him a garland, as being forsaken, or to bind him up a rod, as being worthy to be whipped.

DON PEDRO   To be whipped! What's his fault?

BENEDICK   The flat transgression of a schoolboy, who, being   215
overjoyed with finding a bird's nest, shows it his
companion, and he steals it.

DON PEDRO   Wilt thou make a trust a transgression? The
transgression is in the stealer.

BENEDICK   Yet it had not been amiss the rod had been made,   220
and the garland too. For the garland he might
have worn himself, and the rod he might have
bestowed on you, who, as I take it, have stolen
his bird's nest.

DON PEDRO   I will but teach them to sing, and restore them to   225
the owner.

BENEDICK   If their singing answer your saying, by my faith,
you say honestly.

DON PEDRO   The Lady Beatrice hath a quarrel to you. The
gentleman that danced with her told her she is   230
much wronged by you.

BENEDICK   O, she misused me past the endurance of a
block! An oak but with one green leaf on it
would have answered her; my very visor began
to assume life and scold with her. She told me,   235
not thinking I had been myself, that I was the
Prince's jester, that I was duller than a great thaw;
huddling jest upon jest with such impossible
conveyance upon me that I stood like a man at
a mark, with a whole army shooting at me. She   240
speaks poniards and every word stabs. If her
breath were as terrible as her terminations, there
were no living near her — she would infect to
the north star. I would not marry her, though she
were endowed with all that Adam had left him   245
before he transgressed. She would have made
Hercules have turned spit, yea, and have cleft his
club to make the fire too. Come, talk not of her
— you shall find her the infernal Ate in good
apparel. I would to God some scholar would   250
conjure her, for certainly, while she is here, a man
may live as quiet in hell as in a sanctuary, and
people sin upon purpose, because they would
go thither; so, indeed, all disquiet, horror and
perturbation follows her.   255

Enter CLAUDIO, BEATRICE,
HERO, *and* LEONATO

DON PEDRO   Look, here she comes.

BENEDICK   Will your grace command me any service to

---

215 'transgression' means 'wrong-doing'.

218 'Are you calling honesty a wrong-doing?'

Theme — Loyalty

Don Pedro never had any intention of 'stealing' Hero from Claudio — he is a loyal friend.

232-235 'She would have tested the patience of a block! A dying oak tree would have been provoked by her — my mask was on the verge of arguing with her.'

237 During the spring thaw, roads were blocked with mud and it was impossible to travel.

Character — Benedick

Benedick speaks harshly about Beatrice. The war imagery shows how much her words have hurt him.

239 'conveyance' means 'speed'.

241 'poniards' means 'daggers'.

242 'terminations' means 'words'.

244-246 'even if she was as rich as Adam before he sinned and left paradise'.

246-248 'If she'd been Hercules' wife, she would have made him do chores like turning the meat-spit, and would have broken up his club to feed the fire.'

249 Ate was the goddess of discord in Greek mythology.

255 'perturbation' means 'annoyance' or 'misery'.

Act 2, Scene 1

259 'Antipodes' means 'other side of the world'.

262 'Prester John' was a mythical Christian king of a country in Asia.

263 'great Cham' was Great Khan, ruler of the Mongol empire.

263 'embassage' means 'trip'.

Shakespeare's Techniques

Benedick's <u>language</u> is very <u>insulting</u> — a <u>modern</u> <u>audience</u> might find this <u>offensive</u> rather than <u>funny</u>.

Theme — Love and Marriage

Shakespeare hints that Beatrice had a <u>relationship</u> with Benedick in the <u>past</u>, but she was <u>hurt</u> by him.

277 'You have upset him'.

279-280 Beatrice deliberately misunderstands Don Pedro's phrase 'put down' as 'laid down in bed' and makes a sexual joke.

282 'Wherefore' means 'why'.

Shakespeare's Techniques

Beatrice calls Claudio <u>bitter</u> by making a <u>pun</u> — 'civil as an orange' <u>sounds</u> <u>like</u> '<u>Seville orange</u>' (oranges from Seville were known for being bitter).

289 'blazon' means 'description'.

290 'if Claudio is jealous, he doesn't need to be.'

299-300 'Silence is the best sign of joy. I wouldn't be very happy if I could say how happy I was.'

	the world's end? I will go on the slightest errand now to the Antipodes that you can devise to send me on. I will fetch you a tooth-picker now from the furthest inch of Asia, bring you the length of Prester John's foot, fetch you a hair off the great Cham's beard, do you any embassage to the Pygmies, rather than hold three words' conference with this harpy. You have no employment for me?	260 265
DON PEDRO	None, but to desire your good company.	
BENEDICK	O God, sir, here's a dish I love not — I cannot endure my Lady Tongue.	
	Exit	
DON PEDRO	Come, lady, come, you have lost the heart of Signior Benedick.	270
BEATRICE	Indeed, my lord, he lent it me awhile, and I gave him use for it, a double heart for his single one. Marry, once before he won it of me with false dice, therefore your grace may well say I have lost it.	275
DON PEDRO	You have put him down, lady, you have put him down.	
BEATRICE	So I would not he should do me, my lord, lest I should prove the mother of fools. I have brought Count Claudio, whom you sent me to seek.	280
DON PEDRO	Why, how now, count! Wherefore are you sad?	
CLAUDIO	Not sad, my lord.	
DON PEDRO	How then? Sick?	
CLAUDIO	Neither, my lord.	285
BEATRICE	The count is neither sad, nor sick, nor merry, nor well, but civil count, civil as an orange, and something of that jealous complexion.	
DON PEDRO	I' faith, lady, I think your blazon to be true, though, I'll be sworn, if he be so, his conceit is false. Here, Claudio, I have wooed in thy name, and fair Hero is won. I have broke with her father, and his good will obtained. Name the day of marriage, and God give thee joy!	290
LEONATO	Count, take of me my daughter, and with her my fortunes. His grace hath made the match, and all grace say Amen to it.	295
BEATRICE	Speak, count — 'tis your cue.	
CLAUDIO	Silence is the perfectest herald of joy. I were but little happy, if I could say how much. Lady, as you are mine, I am yours. I give away myself for you and dote upon the exchange.	300
BEATRICE	Speak, cousin, or, if you cannot, stop his mouth with a kiss, and let not him speak neither.	

Act 2, Scene 1

DON PEDRO	In faith, lady, you have a merry heart.	305
BEATRICE	Yea, my lord, I thank it — poor fool, it keeps on the windy side of care. My cousin tells him in his ear that he is in her heart.	
CLAUDIO	And so she doth, cousin.	
BEATRICE	Good Lord, for alliance! Thus goes every one to the world but I, and I am sunburnt. I may sit in a corner and cry heigh-ho for a husband!	310
DON PEDRO	Lady Beatrice, I will get you one.	
BEATRICE	I would rather have one of your father's getting. Hath your grace ne'er a brother like you? Your father got excellent husbands, if a maid could come by them.	315
DON PEDRO	Will you have me, lady?	
BEATRICE	No, my lord, unless I might have another for working-days: your grace is too costly to wear every day. But, I beseech your grace, pardon me — I was born to speak all mirth and no matter.	320
DON PEDRO	Your silence most offends me, and to be merry best becomes you, for, out of question, you were born in a merry hour.	325
BEATRICE	No, sure, my lord, my mother cried, but then there was a star danced, and under that was I born. Cousins — God give you joy!	
LEONATO	Niece, will you look to those things I told you of?	
BEATRICE	I cry you mercy, uncle. By your grace's pardon.	330
	Exit	
DON PEDRO	By my troth, a pleasant-spirited lady.	
LEONATO	There's little of the melancholy element in her, my lord. She is never sad but when she sleeps, and not ever sad then, for I have heard my daughter say, she hath often dreamed of unhappiness and waked herself with laughing.	335
DON PEDRO	She cannot endure to hear tell of a husband.	
LEONATO	O, by no means — she mocks all her wooers out of suit.	
DON PEDRO	She were an excellent wife for Benedick.	340
LEONATO	O Lord, my lord, if they were but a week married, they would talk themselves mad.	
DON PEDRO	County Claudio, when mean you to go to church?	
CLAUDIO	To-morrow, my lord — time goes on crutches till love have all his rites.	345
LEONATO	Not till Monday, my dear son, which is hence a just seven-night, and a time too brief, too, to have all things answer my mind.	
DON PEDRO	Come, you shake the head at so long a breathing — but, I warrant thee, Claudio, the time shall not	350

306-307 'it stays out of care's way'.

Character — Beatrice

Beatrice jokingly pretends to be upset that everyone is getting married apart from her. This could emphasise how uninterested she is in finding a husband.

Theme — Honour and Reputation

Beatrice says that she couldn't marry Don Pedro because his social status is higher than hers. She shows this by using a clothing metaphor.

322 'mirth' means 'amusement'.

Character — Don Pedro

Don Pedro enjoys matchmaking — as soon as he has wooed Hero for Claudio, he decides to set up Benedick and Beatrice.

345 'rites' means 'customs'.

346-347 'a just seven-night' is 'a full week'.

349 'breathing' means 'wait' or 'pause'.

Act Two

Act 2, Scene 1

352 Hercules was a Greek hero who had to perform twelve near-impossible tasks ('labours').

354-357 'I'd like to see them married, and I'm sure I can pull it off, if you three give me the help I ask for.'

358-359 'ten nights' watchings' means 'ten sleepless nights'.

go dully by us. I will in the interim undertake one of Hercules' labours, which is, to bring Signior Benedick and the Lady Beatrice into a mountain of affection the one with the other. I would fain have it a match, and I doubt not but to fashion it, if you three will but minister such assistance as I shall give you direction.   355

LEONATO   My lord, I am for you, though it cost me ten nights' watchings.

CLAUDIO   And I, my lord.   360

DON PEDRO   And you too, gentle Hero?

HERO   I will do any modest office, my lord, to help my cousin to a good husband.

DON PEDRO   And Benedick is not the unhopefullest husband that I know. Thus far can I praise him — he is of a noble strain, of approved valour and confirmed honesty. I will teach you how to humour your cousin, that she shall fall in love with Benedick; and I, with your two helps, will so practise on Benedick that, in despite of his quick wit and his queasy stomach, he shall fall in love with Beatrice. If we can do this, Cupid is no longer an archer: his glory shall be ours, for we are the only love-gods. Go in with me, and I will tell you my drift.   365   370   375

Exeunt

Shakespeare's Techniques

Don Pedro's plan <u>drives</u> the <u>plot</u> of the play. It creates <u>anticipation</u> for the audience — they expect there will be <u>humour</u> and <u>romance</u> to look forward to.

Shakespeare's Techniques

Don Pedro uses <u>classical imagery</u> to describe his plan. This makes it sound <u>noble</u> and <u>dramatic</u> — he says they will have Cupid's "<u>glory</u>" if they succeed.

Theme — Love and Marriage

Claudio is presented as a <u>typical courtly lover</u> — he follows a <u>traditional</u> approach to courtship by <u>wooing</u> Hero even though they <u>don't know</u> each other very well. He is <u>madly</u> in <u>love</u>, but also <u>jealous</u> and <u>immature</u> — he quickly <u>gives up</u> on Hero when he thinks Don Pedro wants to marry her. Through Claudio, Shakespeare <u>mocks</u> the <u>courtly love</u> tradition by suggesting it's based on feelings that are <u>superficial</u> and <u>changeable</u>.

In contrast, Benedick and Beatrice <u>reject love</u> and <u>marriage</u> at first — their <u>relationship</u> will develop in a very <u>different</u> way to Claudio and Hero's.

© Geraint Lewis / Alamy Stock Photo

Act 2, Scene 2 — Borachio Suggests a New Plan

Don John is still determined to <u>ruin</u> Claudio and Hero's <u>relationship</u>.
Borachio suggests a plan to make Claudio think Hero has been <u>unfaithful</u>.

Photo by Reg Wilson © RSC.

ACT 2, SCENE 2

> A HALL IN LEONATO'S HOUSE
>
> *Enter* DON JOHN *and* BORACHIO
>
> DON JOHN   It is so — the Count Claudio shall marry the
> daughter of Leonato.
>
> BORACHIO   Yea, my lord, but I can cross it.
>
> DON JOHN   Any bar, any cross, any impediment will be
> medicinable to me. I am sick in displeasure to   5
> him, and whatsoever comes athwart his affection
> ranges evenly with mine. How canst thou cross
> this marriage?
>
> BORACHIO   Not honestly, my lord, but so covertly that no
> dishonesty shall appear in me.   10
>
> DON JOHN   Show me briefly how.
>
> BORACHIO   I think I told your lordship a year since, how
> much I am in the favour of Margaret, the waiting
> gentlewoman to Hero.
>
> DON JOHN   I remember.   15
>
> BORACHIO   I can, at any unseasonable instant of the night,
> appoint her to look out at her lady's chamber
> window.
>
> DON JOHN   What life is in that, to be the death of this
> marriage?   20
>
> BORACHIO   The poison of that lies in you to temper. Go you
> to the Prince your brother; spare not to tell him
> that he hath wronged his honour in marrying the
> renowned Claudio — whose estimation do you
> mightily hold up — to a contaminated stale, such   25
> a one as Hero.
>
> DON JOHN   What proof shall I make of that?
>
> BORACHIO   Proof enough to misuse the prince, to vex
> Claudio, to undo Hero and kill Leonato. Look you
> for any other issue?   30
>
> DON JOHN   Only to despite them, I will endeavour any thing.
>
> BORACHIO   Go, then, find me a meet hour to draw Don Pedro
> and the Count Claudio alone. Tell them that you
> know that Hero loves me, intend a kind of zeal
> both to the Prince and Claudio (as in love of your   35
> brother's honour, who hath made this match,
> and his friend's reputation, who is thus like to be
> cozened with the semblance of a maid) that you
> have discovered thus. They will scarcely believe
> this without trial — offer them instances, which   40
> shall bear no less likelihood than to see me at her

3 'cross' means 'prevent'.

4-7 'Anything that gets in the way of the marriage will be good for me. I am fed up of Claudio, and whatever upsets him, suits me.'

16 'at any time of night, no matter how late'.

Theme — Honour and Reputation

Borachio knows that Don Pedro and Claudio will want to <u>protect</u> their <u>reputations</u> — he uses this to <u>manipulate</u> them.

21 'How you use this to cause trouble is up to you.'

24-25 'who you think is a marvellous chap'.

25 'contaminated stale' means 'disgraced woman'.

30 'issue' means 'result'.

Shakespeare's Techniques

Borachio uses <u>imperatives</u> (<u>commanding verbs</u>) — the <u>plan</u> is his <u>idea</u> and he is in <u>control</u> of it. Don John <u>isn't</u> a very <u>effective villain</u> — he needs Borachio's help.

34 'pretend to be really upset'.

37-38 'who's going to be fooled by someone who only seems to be a virgin'.

40 'instances' means 'proof'.

Act Two

Act 2, Scene 3 — Benedick is Deceived

chamber-window, hear me call Margaret Hero,
hear Margaret term me Claudio, and bring them
to see this the very night before the intended
wedding. For in the meantime I will so fashion the 45
matter that Hero shall be absent, and there shall
appear such seeming truth of Hero's disloyalty
that jealousy shall be called assurance and all the
preparation overthrown.

48-49 'jealousy will take the place of evidence, and all the wedding plans will be cancelled.'

50-51 'I don't care what the results will be, I'm going to see this through.'

Character — Borachio

Borachio is a clever villain — he suggests a cunning plan and uses Don John to earn money for himself.

DON JOHN	Grow this to what adverse issue it can, I will put it in practice. Be cunning in the working this, and thy fee is a thousand ducats.	50
BORACHIO	Be you constant in the accusation, and my cunning shall not shame me.	
DON JOHN	I will presently go learn their day of marriage.	55

Exeunt

Benedick thinks Claudio is a fool for falling in love. He hides in the orchard and overhears Don Pedro, Claudio and Leonato talking about how Beatrice is in love with him. He falls for their trick.

ACT 2, SCENE 3

Shakespeare's Techniques

An orchard can symbolise fruitfulness and new life — this could suggest that the plan will be successful, or even hint at a marriage.

LEONATO'S ORCHARD

Enter BENEDICK

| BENEDICK | Boy! |
| | *Enter* BOY |

4 'hither' means 'here'.

6 'hence' means 'away from here'.

BOY	Signior?
BENEDICK	In my chamber-window lies a book — bring it hither to me in the orchard.
BOY	I am here already, sir.	5
BENEDICK	I know that, but I would have thee hence, and here again.

Shakespeare's Techniques

Benedick is alone on stage — his soliloquy (lines 8-38) allows him to share his thoughts with the audience without other characters hearing him.

Exit BOY

I do much wonder that one man — seeing how
much another man is a fool when he dedicates
his behaviours to love — will, after he hath 10
laughed at such shallow follies in others, become
the argument of his own scorn by falling in love;
and such a man is Claudio. I have known when
there was no music with him but the drum and the
fife, and now had he rather hear the tabor and the 15
pipe. I have known when he would have walked
ten mile a-foot to see a good armour; and now
will he lie ten nights awake, carving the fashion of
a new doublet. He was wont to speak plain and
to the purpose, like an honest man and a soldier; 20

how do guys make fun of love then be in it

11-12 'become the exact thing he once criticised'.

13-16 'I remember when he only had ears for military music, now he only cares about courtly music.'

19 A 'doublet' was a type of jacket worn in Shakespeare's time.

19 'He was wont to' means 'he used to'.

Act 2, Scene 3

and now is he turned orthography — his words
are a very fantastical banquet, just so many
strange dishes. May I be so converted and see
with these eyes? I cannot tell — I think not — I
will not be sworn, but love may transform me to   25
an oyster; but I'll take my oath on it, till he have
made an oyster of me, he shall never make me
such a fool. One woman is <u>fair</u>, yet I am well;
another is <u>wise</u>, yet I am well; another <u>virtuous</u>,
yet I am well; but till all <u>graces</u> be in one woman,   30
one woman shall <u>not come in my grace</u>. Rich she
shall be, that's certain; wise, or I'll none; virtuous,
or I'll never cheapen her; fair, or I'll never look
on her; <u>mild</u>, or come not near me; <u>noble</u>, or not
I for an angel; of good <u>discourse</u>, an excellent   35
<u>musician</u>, and her hair shall be of what colour it
please God. Ha! The Prince and Monsieur Love!
I will hide me in the arbour.

could this happen to me

Withdraws

Enter DON PEDRO, CLAUDIO, and LEONATO

DON PEDRO   Come, shall we hear this music?

CLAUDIO   Yea, my good lord. How still the evening is,   40
As hushed on purpose to grace harmony!

DON PEDRO   See you where Benedick hath hid himself?

CLAUDIO   O, very well, my lord. The music ended,
We'll fit the kid-fox with a pennyworth.

Enter BALTHASAR, with music

DON PEDRO   Come, Balthasar, we'll hear that song again.   45

BALTHASAR   O, good my lord, tax not so bad a voice
To slander music any more than once.

DON PEDRO   It is the witness still of excellency
To put a strange face on his own perfection.
I pray thee, sing, and let me woo no more.   50

BALTHASAR   Because you talk of wooing, I will sing,
Since many a wooer doth commence his suit
To her he thinks not worthy, yet he woos,
Yet will he swear he loves.

DON PEDRO   Now, pray thee, come;
Or, if thou wilt hold longer argument,   55
Do it in notes.

BALTHASAR   Note this before my notes;
There's not a note of mine that's worth the noting.

DON PEDRO   Why, these are very crotchets that he speaks —
Note, notes, forsooth, and nothing.

Music

BENEDICK   *(Aside)* Now, divine air! Now is his soul ravished!   60
Is it not strange that sheep's guts should hale
souls out of men's bodies? Well, a horn for my
money, when all's done.

21-23 'and now he talks in a flowery style.'

24-28 'I couldn't swear to it, but love could turn me into an oyster, but I will make an oath that until love does turn me into an oyster, it won't make such a fool out of me.'

Theme — Love and Marriage

Benedick is <u>determined</u> that he will <u>never</u> get <u>married</u> — he says that a woman would have to be <u>perfect</u> to make him fall in <u>love</u>.

35 'discourse' means 'conversation'.

38 An 'arbour' is a shady alcove in a garden.

Stagecraft

When Benedick <u>hides</u>, he must still be <u>visible</u> to the other characters, but he <u>mustn't know</u> that they can <u>see</u> him. He might hide in a <u>tree</u> or behind a <u>bush</u>.

40-41 'What a calm evening, as though it had gone quiet on purpose to make the music sound better!'

43-44 'When the music's over we'll set the fox (Benedick) up for a dodgy deal.'

48-49 'It's a mark of excellence when someone denies that he is perfect.'

55-56 'if you want to carry on arguing, at least do it in a song.'

Shakespeare's Techniques

<u>Puns</u> about <u>musical notes</u> and '<u>noting</u>' (observing) reflect that Benedick is about to <u>observe</u> his friends and be <u>tricked</u> by what he sees.

58 'crotchets' are musical notes, but it can also mean 'silly things'.

61-62 'Isn't it odd that instruments made of sheep's insides can help people express such strong feelings?'

Act Two

3

Act 2, Scene 3

69 'blithe and bonny' means 'happy and good looking'.

Theme — Deception and Misunderstanding

The male characters often don't trust women, but it is the men in the play can't be trusted.

BALTHASAR	*(Sings) Sigh no more, ladies, sigh no more,*	
	Men were deceivers ever,	65
	One foot in sea and one on shore,	
	To one thing constant never;	
	Then sigh not so, but let them go,	
	And be you blithe and bonny,	
	Converting all your sounds of woe	70
	Into hey nonny, nonny.	
	Sing no more ditties, sing no moe,	
	Of dumps so dull and heavy.	
	The fraud of men was ever so,	
	Since summer first was leavy;	75
	Then sigh not so, but let them go,	
	And be you blithe and bonny,	
	Converting all your sounds of woe	
	Into hey nonny, nonny.	
DON PEDRO	By my troth, a good song.	80
BALTHASAR	And an ill singer, my lord.	
DON PEDRO	Ha! No, no, faith! Thou singest well enough for a shift.	

83 'shift' means 'emergency'.

84 'An' means 'if'.

86 'isn't a bad omen'.

87 'lief' means 'gladly'.

| BENEDICK | *(Aside)* An he had been a dog that should have howled thus, they would have hanged him, and I pray God his bad voice bode no mischief. I had as lief have heard the night-raven, come what plague could have come after it. | 85 |

89 'marry' means 'truly'.

DON PEDRO	Yea, marry, dost thou hear, Balthasar? I pray thee, get us some excellent music, for to-morrow night we would have it at the Lady Hero's chamber-window.	90
BALTHASAR	The best I can, my lord.	
DON PEDRO	Do so. Farewell.	
	Exit BALTHASAR	
	Come hither, Leonato. What was it you told me of today, that your niece Beatrice was in love with Signior Benedick?	95

Shakespeare's Techniques

Hunting imagery describes Benedick as prey for the men to catch. It makes the trick seem like a trap for Benedick to fall into.

| CLAUDIO | O ay! *(Aside to Don Pedro)* Stalk on, stalk on, the fowl sits — I did never think that lady would have loved any man. | 100 |

102 'dote on' means 'adore'.

104 'abhor' means 'hate'.

| LEONATO | No, nor I neither, but most wonderful that she should so dote on Signior Benedick, whom she hath in all outward behaviours seemed ever to abhor. | |

105 'Is that the way things are?'

| BENEDICK | *(Aside)* Is't possible? Sits the wind in that corner? | 105 |
| LEONATO | By my troth, my lord, I cannot tell what to think of it but that she loves him with an enraged affection — it is past the infinite of thought. | |

108 'it's beyond all understanding'.

109 'counterfeit' means 'pretend'.

| DON PEDRO | Maybe she doth but counterfeit. | |
| CLAUDIO | Faith, like enough. | 110 |

Act 2, Scene 3

LEONATO	O God, counterfeit! There was never counterfeit of passion came so near the life of passion as she discovers it.
DON PEDRO	Why, what effects of passion shows she?
CLAUDIO	*(Aside)* Bait the hook well — this fish will bite. 115
LEONATO	What effects, my lord? She will sit you, you heard my daughter tell you how.
CLAUDIO	She did, indeed.
DON PEDRO	How, how, pray you? You amaze me. I would have thought her spirit had been invincible 120 against all assaults of affection.
LEONATO	I would have sworn it had, my lord, especially against Benedick.
BENEDICK	*(Aside)* I should think this a gull, but that the white-bearded fellow speaks it. Knavery cannot, 125 sure, hide himself in such reverence.
CLAUDIO	*(Aside)* He hath ta'en the infection. Hold it up.
DON PEDRO	Hath she made her affection known to Benedick?
LEONATO	No, and swears she never will. That's her torment.
CLAUDIO	'Tis true, indeed, so your daughter says. 'Shall I,' 130 says she, 'that have so oft encountered him with scorn, write to him that I love him?'
LEONATO	This says she now when she is beginning to write to him, for she'll be up twenty times a night, and there will she sit in her smock till she have writ a 135 sheet of paper — my daughter tells us all.
CLAUDIO	Now you talk of a sheet of paper, I remember a pretty jest your daughter told us of.
LEONATO	O — when she had writ it and was reading it over, she found Benedick and Beatrice between the 140 sheet?
CLAUDIO	That.
LEONATO	O, she tore the letter into a thousand halfpence, railed at herself, that she should be so immodest to write to one that she knew would flout her. 145 'I measure him,' says she, 'by my own spirit, for I should flout him, if he writ to me, yea, though I love him, I should.'
CLAUDIO	Then down upon her knees she falls, weeps, sobs, beats her heart, tears her hair, prays, 150 curses, 'O sweet Benedick! God give me patience!'
LEONATO	She doth indeed. My daughter says so, and the ecstasy hath so much overborne her that my daughter is sometime afeared she will do a 155 desperate outrage to herself. It is very true.
DON PEDRO	It were good that Benedick knew of it by some other, if she will not discover it.

111-113 'No one can pretend as well as that.'

124 'gull' means 'trick'.

Theme — Honour and Reputation
Benedick thinks Leonato ("the white-bearded fellow") is too respectable to be part of a trick — this makes the deception more believable.

127 'Benedick's fallen for the trick.'

Shakespeare's Techniques
The audience knows that Beatrice hasn't said these things. This dramatic irony adds to the humour when Benedick falls for the trick.

Shakespeare's Techniques
This is a pun — "sheet" refers to the paper the letter was written on, but it also creates a joke saying that Benedick and Beatrice were in bed together.

144 'railed at herself' means 'told herself off'.

145 'flout' means 'reject'.

146 "I'm judging him,' she says 'by my own standards".

154-156 'the strength of her feelings has overpowered her so much that my daughter is sometimes afraid she might even hurt herself.'

158 'discover' means 'reveal'.

Act 2, Scene 3

CLAUDIO	To what end? He would make but a sport of it and torment the poor lady worse.	160
DON PEDRO	And he should, it were an alms to hang him. She's an excellent sweet lady, and, out of all suspicion, she is virtuous.	
CLAUDIO	And she is exceeding wise.	
DON PEDRO	In every thing but in loving Benedick.	165
LEONATO	O, my lord, wisdom and blood combatting in so tender a body, we have ten proofs to one that blood hath the victory. I am sorry for her, as I have just cause, being her uncle and her guardian.	170
DON PEDRO	I would she had bestowed this dotage on me: I would have daffed all other respects and made her half myself. I pray you, tell Benedick of it, and hear what a' will say.	
LEONATO	Were it good, think you?	175
CLAUDIO	Hero thinks surely she will die, for she says she will die, if he love her not, and she will die, ere she make her love known, and she will die, if he woo her, rather than she will bate one breath of her accustomed crossness.	180
DON PEDRO	She doth well. If she should make tender of her love, 'tis very possible he'll scorn it, for the man, as you know all, hath a contemptible spirit.	
CLAUDIO	He is a very proper man.	
DON PEDRO	He hath indeed a good outward happiness.	185
CLAUDIO	Before God! — and, in my mind, very wise.	
DON PEDRO	He doth indeed show some sparks that are like wit.	
CLAUDIO	And I take him to be valiant.	
DON PEDRO	As Hector, I assure you, and in the managing of quarrels you may say he is wise, for either he avoids them with great discretion, or undertakes them with a most Christian-like fear.	190
LEONATO	If he do fear God, a' must necessarily keep peace: if he break the peace, he ought to enter into a quarrel with fear and trembling.	195
DON PEDRO	And so will he do, for the man doth fear God, howsoever it seems not in him by some large jests he will make. Well, I am sorry for your niece. Shall we go seek Benedick, and tell him of her love?	200
CLAUDIO	Never tell him, my lord. Let her wear it out with good counsel.	
LEONATO	Nay, that's impossible — she may wear her heart out first.	
DON PEDRO	Well, we will hear further of it by your daughter. Let it cool the while. I love Benedick well, and I	205

161 'If he did, it would be best to hang him.'

166-168 'Oh, my lord, when wisdom and passion compete in such a tender body, it's ten to one that passion will succeed.'

171-173 'I wish it was me she had given her heart to: I would have set aside all other considerations and married her.'

Theme — Love and Marriage

Shakespeare exaggerates the effects of lovesick behaviour — he is mocking traditional courtly lovers.

179 'bate' means 'hold back'.

Character — Don Pedro

Don Pedro knows that Benedick can hear what they're saying and so he can't resist insulting him.

183 'contemptible' means 'hateful'.

189 In Greek mythology, Hector was a hero in the Trojan War, known for his courage.

191 'discretion' means 'care'.

197-198 'even though his joking makes it seem like he doesn't'.

201-202 'Let her get over it with the help of good advice.'

Act 2, Scene 3

could wish he would modestly examine himself, to see how much he is unworthy so good a lady.

LEONATO	My lord, will you walk? Dinner is ready.	
CLAUDIO	*(Aside)* If he do not dote on her upon this, I will never trust my expectation.	210
DON PEDRO	*(Aside)* Let there be the same net spread for her, and that must your daughter and her gentlewomen carry. The sport will be when they hold one an opinion of another's dotage, and no such matter. That's the scene that I would see, which will be merely a dumb-show. Let us send her to call him in to dinner.	215

Exeunt DON PEDRO, CLAUDIO *and* LEONATO

BENEDICK	*(Coming forward)* This can be no trick. The conference was sadly borne. They have the truth of this from Hero. They seem to pity the lady: it seems her affections have their full bent. Love me! Why, it must be requited. I hear how I am censured. They say I will bear myself proudly, if I perceive the love come from her. They say too that she will rather die than give any sign of affection. I did never think to marry. I must not seem proud: happy are they that hear their detractions and can put them to mending. They say the lady is fair — 'tis a truth, I can bear them witness; and virtuous — 'tis so, I cannot reprove it; and wise, but for loving me — by my troth, it is no addition to her wit, nor no great argument of her folly, for I will be horribly in love with her. I may chance have some odd quirks and remnants of wit broken on me, because I have railed so long against marriage, but doth not the appetite alter? A man loves the meat in his youth that he cannot endure in his age. Shall quips and sentences and these paper bullets of the brain awe a man from the career of his humour? No, the world must be peopled. When I said I would die a bachelor, I did not think I should live till I were married. Here comes Beatrice. By this day she's a fair lady! I do spy some marks of love in her.	220 225 230 235 240 245

Enter BEATRICE

BEATRICE	Against my will I am sent to bid you come in to dinner.	
BENEDICK	Fair Beatrice, I thank you for your pains.	
BEATRICE	I took no more pains for those thanks than you take pains to thank me. If it had been painful, I would not have come.	250
BENEDICK	You take pleasure then in the message?	

Side notes:

212-217 'The same trap must be set for Beatrice, and Hero and her servants must do it. The fun will start when they both believe the other one's in love with them. That's the scene I want to see — it'll be no more than a puppet show.'

Shakespeare's Techniques

Benedick has another soliloquy about love — the men's trick has made him change his mind about love and Beatrice since the start of the scene.

222 'have their full bent' means 'are in full flow'.

224 'censured' means 'criticised'.

228-229 'it's a good thing to take criticism on board.'

231 'reprove' means 'contradict'.

Theme — Love and Marriage

Fair, virtuous and wise is how Benedick described his ideal woman in lines 28-37. Now that he thinks Beatrice loves him, he sees those qualities in her.

234-238 'People might tease me and make jokes about me, because I've criticised marriage for so long, but don't tastes change?'

239-241 'Should jokes and insults be allowed to scare a man away from what he really wants to do?'

(Handwritten notes: "→ respects hero" · "- benedick is not impressed with outward appearances" · "- in movie all men are slanting hero, benedick is with hero")

Act Two — Practice Questions

254-256 'About as much pleasure as you can fit on a knife point and choke a jackdaw with. You're not hungry'.

BEATRICE	Yea, just so much as you may take upon a knife's point and choke a daw withal. You have no stomach, signior. Fare you well.	255
	Exit	
BENEDICK	Ha! 'Against my will I am sent to bid you come in to dinner,' — there's a double meaning in that. 'I took no more pains for those thanks than you took pains to thank me,' — that's as much as to say, 'Any pains that I take for you is as easy as thanks.' If I do not take pity of her, I am a villain; if I do not love her, I am a Jew. I will go get her picture.	260
	Exit	

Character — Benedick

Benedick <u>misunderstands</u> Beatrice's <u>normal behaviour</u> — he is <u>convinced</u> that she <u>loves</u> him and thinks she is dropping <u>hints</u> about it.

263 In Elizabethan times, it was a common prejudice that Jews were selfish and not to be trusted.

Quick Questions

1) What does Don John tell Claudio at the masked ball?

2) Who suggests the plan to bring Benedick and Beatrice together?

3) Explain Borachio's plan to ruin Claudio and Hero's relationship.

4) Which character sings a song about deception?

5) Where is Benedick when he is tricked by his friends?

In-depth Questions

1) How are Hero and Beatrice presented as opposites in Act 2, Scene 1?

2) How does Shakespeare create a light-hearted mood at the masked ball?

3) Describe how Claudio is presented in Act 2, Scene 1.
   How do you think the audience might respond to him in this scene?

4) Compare the reasons that Benedick and Beatrice give for disliking marriage.

5) Why do you think Shakespeare gives Benedick two soliloquies in Act 2, Scene 3?

6) What techniques does Shakespeare use to create humour when the men trick Benedick?

Act 3, Scene 1 — Beatrice is Deceived

It's Beatrice's turn to be <u>tricked</u>. She <u>overhears</u> Hero and Ursula saying Benedick's in <u>love</u> with her and <u>believes</u> every word.

© Donald Cooper / REX / Shutterstock

ACT 3, SCENE 1

LEONATO'S GARDEN

Enter HERO, MARGARET *and* URSULA

HERO	Good Margaret, run thee to the parlour —
	There shalt thou find my cousin Beatrice
	Proposing with the Prince and Claudio.
	Whisper her ear and tell her, I and Ursula
	Walk in the orchard and our whole discourse 5
	Is all of her. Say that thou overheard'st us,
	And bid her steal into the pleached bower,
	Where honeysuckles, ripened by the sun,
	Forbid the sun to enter, like favourites,
	Made proud by princes, that advance their pride 10
	Against that power that bred it. **There will she hide her,**
	To listen our purpose. This is thy office —
	Bear thee well in it and leave us alone.
MARGARET	I'll make her come, I warrant you, presently.

Exit

HERO	Now, Ursula, when Beatrice doth come, 15
	As we do trace this alley up and down,
	Our talk must only be of Benedick.
	When I do name him, let it be thy part
	To praise him more than ever man did merit.
	My talk to thee must be how Benedick 20
	Is sick in love with Beatrice. Of this matter
	Is little Cupid's crafty arrow made,
	That only wounds by hearsay.

Enter BEATRICE, *behind*

	Now begin,
	For look where Beatrice, like a lapwing, runs
	Close by the ground, to hear our conference. 25
URSULA	The pleasant'st angling is to see the fish
	Cut with her golden oars the silver stream,
	And greedily devour the treacherous bait.
	So angle we for Beatrice, who even now
	Is couched in the woodbine coverture. 30
	Fear you not my part of the dialogue.
HERO	Then go we near her, that her ear lose nothing
	Of the false-sweet bait that we lay for it.

(Approaching the bower)

	No, truly, Ursula, she is too disdainful.
	I know her spirits are as coy and wild 35
	As haggards of the rock.

3 'Proposing' means 'talking'.

7 'steal' means 'sneak'.

7 A 'pleached bower' is a shady shelter made of intertwined branches.

9-11 'like a prince's favourites, who become proud, and then use their pride against the power that encouraged it in the first place.'

12 'office' means 'job'.

16 'trace' means 'walk'.

Shakespeare's Techniques

The <u>tricks</u> in Act 2, Scene 3 and Act 3, Scene 1 <u>mirror</u> each other. This <u>structure</u> allows the audience to <u>compare</u> how Benedick and Beatrice <u>react</u> to the tricks.

23 'hearsay' means 'rumour'.

24 A 'lapwing' is a type of bird that flies in jerky movements close to the ground.

Shakespeare's Techniques

<u>Fishing imagery</u> makes the trick seem like an <u>enjoyable</u> sport. It links to the <u>hunting imagery</u> used in Act 2, Scene 3.

30-31 'Is hiding in the honeysuckle bower. Don't worry about my end of the conversation.'

36 A 'haggard' is an untamed hawk.

Act 3, Scene 1

38 'new-trothed' means 'newly engaged'.

40 'They begged me to tell her about it'.

44-46 'Doesn't he deserve to be as lucky as the bed that has Beatrice lie on it?'

Character — Hero

Hero is <u>witty</u> and has <u>more lines</u> than in other scenes. She <u>enjoys</u> the trick and even <u>criticises</u> Beatrice. She's more <u>confident</u> when there are <u>no men</u> around.

52 'Misprising' means 'undervaluing'.

56 'self-endeared' means 'full of herself.'

58 'make sport at it' means 'make fun of it'.

61 'find fault with him'.

63-70 'If he's dark-skinned, she'll say Nature was drawing a caricature and smudged the ink; if he's tall, he's an ugly-headed spear; if he's short, a badly cut gemstone; if he's talkative, she'll say he's like a weather vane, blown by all the winds; and if he's quiet, she'll say he's a block. She turns every man inside out, and never gives credit where it's due.'

71 'carping' means 'criticism'.

72 'from all fashions' means 'contrary'.

77 She's describing a fire that doesn't burn brightly but burns very hot (e.g. a fire in a closed stove).

URSULA	But are you sure That Benedick loves Beatrice so entirely?
HERO	So says the Prince and my new-trothed lord.
URSULA	And did they bid you tell her of it, madam?
HERO	They did entreat me to acquaint her of it, 40 But I persuaded them, if they loved Benedick, To wish him wrestle with affection, And never to let Beatrice know of it.
URSULA	Why did you so? Doth not the gentleman Deserve as full as fortunate a bed 45 As ever Beatrice shall couch upon?
HERO	O god of love! I know he doth deserve As much as may be yielded to a man, But Nature never framed a woman's heart Of prouder stuff than that of Beatrice. 50 Disdain and scorn ride sparkling in her eyes, Misprising what they look on, and her wit Values itself so highly that to her All matter else seems weak. She cannot love, Nor take no shape nor project of affection, 55 She is so self-endeared.
URSULA	Sure, I think so, And therefore certainly it were not good She knew his love, lest she make sport at it.
HERO	Why, you speak truth. I never yet saw man, How wise, how noble, young, how rarely featured, 60 But she would spell him backward. If fair-faced, She would swear the gentleman should be her sister; If black, why, Nature, drawing of an antic, Made a foul blot; if tall, a lance ill-headed; If low, an agate very vilely cut; 65 If speaking, why, a vane blown with all winds; If silent, why, a block moved with none. So turns she every man the wrong side out And never gives to truth and virtue that Which simpleness and merit purchaseth. 70
URSULA	Sure, sure, such carping is not commendable.
HERO	No, not to be so odd and from all fashions As Beatrice is, cannot be commendable: But who dare tell her so? If I should speak, She would mock me into air. O, she would laugh me 75 Out of myself, press me to death with wit. Therefore let Benedick, like covered fire, Consume away in sighs, waste inwardly. It were a better death than die with mocks, Which is as bad as die with tickling. 80
URSULA	Yet tell her of it — hear what she will say.
HERO	No. Rather I will go to Benedick

Act 3, Scene 1

	And counsel him to fight against his passion.
	And, truly, I'll devise some honest slanders
	To stain my cousin with. One doth not know 85
	How much an ill word may empoison liking.
URSULA	O, do not do your cousin such a wrong.
	She cannot be so much without true judgment —
	Having so swift and excellent a wit
	As she is prized to have — as to refuse 90
	So rare a gentleman as Signior Benedick.
HERO	He is the only man of Italy,
	Always excepted my dear Claudio.
URSULA	I pray you, be not angry with me, madam,
	Speaking my fancy: Signior Benedick, 95
	For shape, for bearing, argument and valour,
	Goes foremost in report through Italy.
HERO	Indeed, he hath an excellent good name.
URSULA	His excellence did earn it, ere he had it.
	When are you married, madam? 100
HERO	Why, every day, to-morrow. Come, go in.
	I'll show thee some attires, and have thy counsel
	Which is the best to furnish me to-morrow.
URSULA	(Aside) She's limed, I warrant you:
	we have caught her, madam.
HERO	(Aside) If it prove so, then loving goes by haps; 105
	Some Cupid kills with arrows, some with traps.
	Exeunt HERO *and* URSULA
BEATRICE	(Coming forward)
	What fire is in mine ears? Can this be true?
	Stand I condemned for pride and scorn so much?
	Contempt, farewell, and maiden pride, adieu!
	No glory lives behind the back of such. 110
	And, Benedick, love on. I will requite thee,
	Taming my wild heart to thy loving hand.
	If thou dost love, my kindness shall incite thee
	To bind our loves up in a holy band;
	For others say thou dost deserve, and I 115
	Believe it better than reportingly.
	Exit

Shakespeare's Techniques

Hero talks about how <u>easy</u> it is to <u>ruin</u> someone's <u>reputation</u> by saying <u>bad things</u> about them. This <u>foreshadows</u> her own reputation being ruined by Claudio.

92 'He's the best man in Italy'.

97 'foremost' means 'first'.

102 'attires' means 'outfits'.

104 'limed' means 'caught'. Bird-lime is a sticky substance used to trap birds.

105 'If it turns out that way, then you never know how love might happen'.

Character — Beatrice

In this <u>soliloquy</u>, Beatrice behaves <u>differently</u> — she speaks <u>seriously</u> and <u>questions</u> herself. This reflects how she wants to <u>change</u> for Benedick.

113-116 'If you love me, I'll be nice to you and we can get married — for others say you are worthy and I think they're right.'

Shakespeare's Techniques — Poetry and Prose

The play is mostly written in <u>prose</u>, which makes it <u>unusual</u> — Shakespeare's plays normally contain more <u>verse</u>.

- <u>Prose</u> is like <u>normal speech</u>. Characters like <u>Benedick</u> and <u>Beatrice</u> mostly speak in prose — it suits their <u>fast-paced</u>, <u>witty</u> dialogue.

- Act 3, Scene 1 is written in <u>blank verse</u> — a type of poetry that <u>doesn't rhyme</u>. Each line has around <u>10 syllables</u> with <u>5 stressed syllables</u>: "Stand <u>I</u> con<u>demned</u> for <u>pride</u> and <u>scorn</u> so <u>much</u>?"

- <u>Verse</u> is often used to make a scene more <u>dramatic</u> and <u>serious</u> (e.g. here, and in Act 4, Scene 1, when Hero is <u>accused</u>) or to represent <u>courtly love</u> (e.g. Claudio often speaks in verse when describing his <u>love</u> for Hero).

© Donald Cooper / photostage

Act Three

Act 3, Scene 2 — Don John Deceives Claudio

Photograph by Alastair Muir

Benedick is acting <u>differently</u>. He says it's because he has <u>toothache</u>, but Don Pedro, Claudio and Leonato <u>tease</u> him about being in <u>love</u>. Don John tells Claudio that Hero is being <u>unfaithful</u> to him.

ACT 3, SCENE 2

A ROOM IN LEONATO'S HOUSE

Enter DON PEDRO, CLAUDIO, BENEDICK *and* LEONATO

DON PEDRO	I do but stay till your marriage be consummate, and then go I toward Aragon.
CLAUDIO	I'll bring you thither, my lord, if you'll vouchsafe me.
DON PEDRO	Nay, that would be as great a soil in the new gloss of your marriage as to show a child his new coat and forbid him to wear it. I will only be bold with Benedick for his company; for, from the crown of his head to the sole of his foot, he is all mirth. He hath twice or thrice cut Cupid's bow-string and the little hangman dare not shoot at him. He hath a heart as sound as a bell and his tongue is the clapper, for what his heart thinks his tongue speaks.
BENEDICK	Gallants, I am not as I have been.
LEONATO	So say I — methinks you are sadder.
CLAUDIO	I hope he be in love.
DON PEDRO	Hang him, truant! There's no true drop of blood in him, to be truly touched with love. If he be sad, he wants money.
BENEDICK	I have the toothache.
DON PEDRO	Draw it.
BENEDICK	Hang it!
CLAUDIO	You must hang it first, and draw it afterwards.
DON PEDRO	What! Sigh for the toothache?
LEONATO	Where is but a humour or a worm.
BENEDICK	Well, every one can master a grief but he that has it.
CLAUDIO	Yet say I, he is in love.
DON PEDRO	There is no appearance of fancy in him, unless it be a fancy that he hath to strange disguises; as, to be a Dutchman today, a Frenchman tomorrow, or in the shape of two countries at once, as, a German from the waist downward, all slops, and a Spaniard from the hip upward, no doublet. Unless he have a fancy to this foolery, as it appears he hath, he is no fool for fancy, as you would have it appear he is.
CLAUDIO	If he be not in love with some woman, there is no believing old signs. A' brushes his hat o'

Line numbers: 5, 10, 15, 20, 25, 30, 35

---

3 'I'll go with you if you want.'

4 'gloss' means 'shine'.

9-10 'He's avoided love so much that Cupid's fed up of trying.'

12 A 'clapper' is the bit inside a bell that hits the sides to make it sound.

Character — Benedick

Benedick is <u>quieter</u> and more <u>serious</u> than usual. His friends know it's because he is in <u>love</u>, so they <u>tease</u> him.

14 'Gallants' means 'gentlemen'.

17 'Come on, man!'

Shakespeare's Techniques

This is a <u>pun</u> on 'hanged, drawn and quartered' — <u>traitors</u> were <u>hanged</u>, then had their <u>guts dragged out</u>, then were <u>cut</u> into <u>quarters</u>.

25 The Elizabethans believed toothache was caused by mysterious gases (humours) or little worms that ate into the teeth.

26-27 'It's easy to rise above problems when they're not yours.'

29-30 'He doesn't seem to be in love, unless it's a love for strange costumes'.

33 'slops' means 'baggy trousers'.

Act 3, Scene 2

	mornings. What should that bode?	40
DON PEDRO	Hath any man seen him at the barber's?	
CLAUDIO	No, but the barber's man hath been seen with him, and the old ornament of his cheek hath already stuffed tennis balls.	
LEONATO	Indeed, he looks younger than he did, by the loss of a beard.	45
DON PEDRO	Nay, a' rubs himself with civet. Can you smell him out by that?	
CLAUDIO	That's as much as to say, the sweet youth's in love.	50
DON PEDRO	The greatest note of it is his melancholy.	
CLAUDIO	And when was he wont to wash his face?	
DON PEDRO	Yea, or to paint himself? For the which, I hear what they say of him.	
CLAUDIO	Nay, but his jesting spirit, which is now crept into a lute-string, and now governed by stops.	55
DON PEDRO	Indeed, that tells a heavy tale for him. Conclude, conclude he is in love.	
CLAUDIO	Nay, but I know who loves him.	
DON PEDRO	That would I know too. I warrant, one that knows him not.	60
CLAUDIO	Yes, and his ill conditions, and, in despite of all, dies for him.	
DON PEDRO	She shall be buried with her face upwards.	
BENEDICK	Yet is this no charm for the toothache. Old signior, walk aside with me. I have studied eight or nine wise words to speak to you, which these hobby-horses must not hear.	65
	Exeunt BENEDICK *and* LEONATO	
DON PEDRO	For my life, to break with him about Beatrice.	
CLAUDIO	'Tis even so. Hero and Margaret have by this played their parts with Beatrice, and then the two bears will not bite one another when they meet.	70
	Enter DON JOHN	
DON JOHN	My lord and brother, God save you!	
DON PEDRO	Good den, brother.	
DON JOHN	If your leisure served, I would speak with you.	75
DON PEDRO	In private?	
DON JOHN	If it please you, yet Count Claudio may hear, for what I would speak of concerns him.	
DON PEDRO	What's the matter?	
DON JOHN	*(To Claudio)* Means your lordship to be married tomorrow?	80
DON PEDRO	You know he does.	

40 'bode' means 'foretell'.

43-44 'his old beard has been used to stuff tennis balls'.

Theme — Love and Marriage

Benedick has shaved and is wearing perfume ("civet") — these are things a courtly lover would do to impress the woman he loved.

52 'wont' means 'accustomed'.

53-54 'Yes, or to wear make-up? That's what people are saying about him.'

55-56 'No, the clearest proof is his sense of humour — he's singing love songs instead of using his wit.'

62 'ill conditions' means 'bad habits'.

Theme — Love and Marriage

Claudio uses a metaphor to show that Benedick and Beatrice have a hostile relationship, but he thinks they will become more gentle now they are in love.

74 'Good den' means 'good afternoon' or 'good evening'.

Act 3, Scene 2

84 'impediment' means 'obstacle'.

85-90 'You'll think better of me when you've heard me out. My brother thinks highly of you, and has helped arrange your marriage — what a waste of time and effort.'

92-93 'to cut a long story short'.

Theme — Gender

Accusing Hero of sleeping with other men is a serious accusation. Elizabethan women were valued for being 'pure' and were expected to stay as virgins until they got married.

101-102 'Don't think any more about it till you've got proof.'

Theme — Honour and Reputation

Don John knows Claudio wouldn't marry a woman if she wasn't a virgin — doing that would damage Claudio's reputation.

109-112 'Don't be so sure until you've seen the evidence. If you come with me, I'll give you proof and you can decide what to do.'

Character — Claudio

Claudio is very quick to doubt Hero. He speaks harshly and shows how suspicious and changeable he can be.

118-120 'I won't say any more against her till you've seen the proof. Keep it to yourselves till midnight, and then let the story come out.'

124 'the sequel' means 'what's next'.

DON JOHN	I know not that, when he knows what I know.
CLAUDIO	If there be any impediment, I pray you discover it.
DON JOHN	You may think I love you not. Let that appear hereafter, and aim better at me by that I now will manifest. For my brother, I think he holds you well, and in dearness of heart hath holp to effect your ensuing marriage — surely suit ill-spent and labour ill-bestowed.
DON PEDRO	Why, what's the matter?
DON JOHN	I came hither to tell you, and, circumstances shortened, for she has been too long a talking of, the lady is disloyal.
CLAUDIO	Who, Hero?
DON JOHN	Even she — Leonato's Hero, your Hero, every man's Hero.
CLAUDIO	Disloyal?
DON JOHN	The word is too good to paint out her wickedness. I could say she were worse; think you of a worse title, and I will fit her to it. Wonder not till further warrant. Go but with me tonight, you shall see her chamber window entered, even the night before her wedding day. If you love her then, tomorrow wed her; but it would better fit your honour to change your mind.
CLAUDIO	May this be so?
DON PEDRO	I will not think it.
DON JOHN	If you dare not trust that you see, confess not that you know. If you will follow me, I will show you enough, and when you have seen more and heard more, proceed accordingly.
CLAUDIO	If I see any thing tonight why I should not marry her, tomorrow in the congregation, where I should wed, there will I shame her.
DON PEDRO	And, as I wooed for thee to obtain her, I will join with thee to disgrace her.
DON JOHN	I will disparage her no farther till you are my witnesses. Bear it coldly but till midnight, and let the issue show itself.
DON PEDRO	O day untowardly turned!
CLAUDIO	O mischief strangely thwarting!
DON JOHN	O plague right well prevented! So will you say when you have seen the sequel.

Exeunt

Act Three

Act 3, Scene 3 — The Watch Make an Arrest

Dogberry and Verges brief the <u>Watch</u> on their night-time guard duties. The Watch overhear Borachio <u>boasting</u> to Conrade about the <u>trick</u> he played on Claudio and Don Pedro.

© Donald Cooper / photostage

ACT 3, SCENE 3

A STREET

Enter DOGBERRY *and* VERGES *with the Watch*

DOGBERRY	Are you good men and true?	
VERGES	Yea, or else it were pity but they should suffer salvation, body and soul.	
DOGBERRY	Nay, that were a punishment too good for them, if they should have any allegiance in them, being chosen for the Prince's Watch.	5
VERGES	Well, give them their charge, neighbour Dogberry.	
DOGBERRY	First, who think you the most desertless man to be constable?	
FIRST WATCHMAN	Hugh Otecake, sir, or George Seacole, for they can write and read.	10
DOGBERRY	Come hither, neighbour Seacole. God hath blessed you with a good name — to be a well-favoured man is the gift of fortune, but to write and read comes by nature.	15
SECOND WATCHMAN	Both which, master constable —	
DOGBERRY	You have — I knew it would be your answer. Well, for your favour, sir, why, give God thanks, and make no boast of it; and for your writing and reading, let that appear when there is no need of such vanity. You are thought here to be the most senseless and fit man for the constable of the Watch — therefore bear you the lantern. This is your charge: you shall comprehend all vagrom men; you are to bid any man stand, in the Prince's name.	20 25
SECOND WATCHMAN	How if a' will not stand?	
DOGBERRY	Why, then, take no note of him, but let him go, and presently call the rest of the Watch together and thank God you are rid of a knave.	30
VERGES	If he will not stand when he is bidden, he is none of the Prince's subjects.	
DOGBERRY	True, and they are to meddle with none but the Prince's subjects. You shall also make no noise in the streets, for, for the Watch to babble and to talk is most tolerable and not to be endured.	35
WATCHMAN	We will rather sleep than talk: we know what belongs to a Watch.	
DOGBERRY	Why, you speak like an ancient and most quiet watchman, for I cannot see how sleeping should	40

3 He means 'damnation'.

7 'charge' means 'orders'.

8 'desertless' means 'undeserving', but Dogberry means 'deserving'.

12-13 Sea coal was good quality coal, imported by ship.

14 'well-favoured' means 'good-looking'.

Shakespeare's Techniques

Dogberry often uses <u>malapropisms</u> — he says a <u>wrong word</u> that <u>sounds like</u> the word he means, e.g. '<u>senseless</u>' (useless) when he means '<u>sensible</u>'.

24 He means 'apprehend'.

25 He means 'vagrant' (beggar).

25 'tell him to stop'.

31 'bidden' means 'ordered'.

Context — The Watch

There wasn't a <u>police force</u> in Elizabethan times, so the <u>Watch</u> were supposed to <u>prevent crimes</u>. They had a reputation for being <u>useless</u>.

Act 3, Scene 3

41 'bills' are the watchmen's weapons (long poles with hooks on the ends).

	offend. Only, have a care that your bills be not stolen. Well, you are to call at all the ale-houses, and bid those that are drunk get them to bed.
WATCHMAN	How if they will not?
DOGBERRY	Why, then, let them alone till they are sober. If they make you not then the better answer, you may say they are not the men you took them for.
WATCHMAN	Well, sir.
DOGBERRY	If you meet a thief, you may suspect him, by virtue of your office, to be no true man, and, for such kind of men, the less you meddle or make with them, why the more is for your honesty.
WATCHMAN	If we know him to be a thief, shall we not lay hands on him?
DOGBERRY	Truly, by your office, you may, but I think they that touch pitch will be defiled. The most peaceable way for you, if you do take a thief, is to let him show himself what he is and steal out of your company.
VERGES	You have been always called a merciful man, partner.
DOGBERRY	Truly, I would not hang a dog by my will, much more a man who hath any honesty in him.
VERGES	If you hear a child cry in the night, you must call to the nurse and bid her still it.
WATCHMAN	How if the nurse be asleep and will not hear us?
DOGBERRY	Why, then, depart in peace, and let the child wake her with crying, for the ewe that will not hear her lamb when it baas will never answer a calf when he bleats.
VERGES	'Tis very true.
DOGBERRY	This is the end of the charge. You, constable, are to present the Prince's own person. If you meet the Prince in the night, you may stay him.
VERGES	Nay, by'r lady, that I think a' cannot.
DOGBERRY	Five shillings to one on't, with any man that knows the statutes, he may stay him! Marry, not without the Prince be willing, for, indeed, the Watch ought to offend no man, and it is an offence to stay a man against his will.
VERGES	By'r lady, I think it be so.
DOGBERRY	Ha, ah, ha! Well, masters, good night. An there be any matter of weight chances, call up me. Keep your fellows' counsels and your own, and good night. Come, neighbour.
WATCHMAN	Well, masters, we hear our charge. Let us go sit here upon the church-bench till two, and then all to bed.

45

50

55

60

65

70

75

80

85

51-52 'the less you have to do with people like that, the more honest you will appear.'

55-56 'You're entitled to arrest him, but you can't touch tar without getting dirty.'

Character — Dogberry

Dogberry is incompetent — he tells the Watch not to bother arresting thieves.

Shakespeare's Techniques

Dogberry's incompetence and self-importance provides humour and lightens the mood of the play after the seriousness of Act 3, Scene 2.

65 'still it' means 'quieten it down'.

72-74 'You, constable, deal with the Prince himself. If you meet the Prince in the night you have the right to detain him.'

75 'by'r lady' means 'by our lady'.

77 'statutes' means 'laws'.

82-84 'If anything important happens, come and get me. Follow your companions' good advice and your own'.

Act 3, Scene 3

DOGBERRY	One word more, honest neighbours. I pray you watch about Signior Leonato's door, for the wedding being there tomorrow, there is a great coil to-night. Adieu: be vigitant, I beseech you.	90

Exeunt DOGBERRY *and* VERGES

Enter BORACHIO *and* CONRADE

BORACHIO	What, Conrade!	
WATCHMAN	*(Aside)* Peace! Stir not.	
BORACHIO	Conrade, I say!	95
CONRADE	Here, man. I am at thy elbow.	
BORACHIO	Mass, and my elbow itched — I thought there would a scab follow.	
CONRADE	I will owe thee an answer for that; and now forward with thy tale.	100
BORACHIO	Stand thee close, then, under this penthouse, for it drizzles rain, and I will, like a true drunkard, utter all to thee.	
WATCHMAN	*(Aside)* Some treason, masters — yet stand close.	
BORACHIO	Therefore know I have earned of Don John a thousand ducats.	105
CONRADE	Is it possible that any villainy should be so dear?	
BORACHIO	Thou shouldst rather ask if it were possible any villainy should be so rich; for when rich villains have need of poor ones, poor ones may make what price they will.	110
CONRADE	I wonder at it.	
BORACHIO	That shows thou art unconfirmed. Thou knowest that the fashion of a doublet, or a hat, or a cloak, is nothing to a man.	115
CONRADE	Yes, it is apparel.	
BORACHIO	I mean, the fashion.	
CONRADE	Yes, the fashion is the fashion.	
BORACHIO	Tush! I may as well say the fool's the fool. But seest thou not what a deformed thief this fashion is?	120
WATCHMAN	*(Aside)* I know that Deformed. A' has been a vile thief this seven year — a' goes up and down like a gentleman. I remember his name.	
BORACHIO	Didst thou not hear somebody?	125
CONRADE	No. 'Twas the vane on the house.	
BORACHIO	Seest thou not, I say, what a deformed thief this fashion is? How giddily a' turns about all the hot bloods between fourteen and five-and-thirty, sometimes fashioning them like Pharaoh's soldiers in the reechy painting, sometime like god Bel's priests in the old church-window, sometime like the shaven Hercules in the smirched	130

Shakespeare's Techniques

This foreshadows the drama that will happen at the wedding (a "coil" is a disturbance).

94 The Watchman is talking to the rest of the Watch, but Borachio and Conrade can't hear him.

97-98 'I say, I had such an itchy elbow — I thought there would be a scab.' A 'scab' is also a low-life criminal. Itches were supposed to be a sign that a bad person was about to turn up.

101 A 'penthouse' is an overhanging roof.

Character — Borachio

Borachio gives away Don John's plot because he's drunk. His name suggests he drinks a lot — it sounds like the Spanish word for drunk, 'borracho'.

104 'don't do anything yet.'

107 'dear' means 'expensive'.

113 'That shows you're inexperienced.'

Theme — Deception and Misunderstanding

The Watchman takes Borachio's words literally and misunderstands what he means — he thinks Borachio's talking about a criminal called Deformed.

129 'hot bloods' are 'fashionable young men'.

130-131 'Pharaoh's soldiers' are the soldiers who chased the Jews when they were escaping from Egypt in the Bible.

131 'reechy' means 'grimy'.

131-132 In the Bible, Bel's priests played a trick on the king to prove their god (Bel) was real. The king had them killed when he found out.

133 'smirched' means 'dirty'.

Act Three

Act 3, Scene 3

135 'massy' means 'big'.

Shakespeare's Techniques

Borachio and Conrade both criticise fashions, saying they change so quickly that people get rid of clothes they've barely worn. This symbolises how quickly characters change their emotions.

145 'I'm telling this story badly'.

Shakespeare's Techniques

The carefully chosen alliterative sounds emphasise how the men have been carefully manipulated by Don John.

Character — Don John

Everyone knows that Don John is a villain — even Borachio, who works for him, suggests he is evil.

153 'possessed' means 'took hold of'.

164-167 'We've found the worst crime ever seen in this republic.'

169 A lock of hair, grown long, so men could tie bits of ribbon in, given them by their girlfriends.

176-177 'We're a valuable catch for these clowns with weapons.'

178 A 'commodity' is something valuable.

worm-eaten tapestry, where his codpiece seems as massy as his club?

CONRADE All this I see, and I see that the fashion wears out more apparel than the man. But art not thou thyself giddy with the fashion too, that thou hast shifted out of thy tale into telling me of the fashion?

BORACHIO Not so, neither. But know that I have tonight wooed Margaret, the lady Hero's gentlewoman, by the name of Hero. She leans me out at her mistress' chamber-window, bids me a thousand times goodnight — I tell this tale vilely — I should first tell thee how the Prince, Claudio and my master, planted and placed and possessed by my master Don John, saw afar off in the orchard this amiable encounter.

CONRADE And thought they Margaret was Hero?

BORACHIO Two of them did, the Prince and Claudio; but the devil my master knew she was Margaret; and partly by his oaths, which first possessed them, partly by the dark night, which did deceive them, but chiefly by my villainy, which did confirm any slander that Don John had made, away went Claudio enraged, swore he would meet her, as he was appointed, next morning at the temple, and there, before the whole congregation, shame her with what he saw o'ernight and send her home again without a husband.

FIRST WATCHMAN We charge you, in the Prince's name, stand!

SECOND WATCHMAN Call up the right master constable. We have here recovered the most dangerous piece of lechery that ever was known in the commonwealth.

FIRST WATCHMAN And one Deformed is one of them. I know him — a' wears a lock.

CONRADE Masters, masters —

SECOND WATCHMAN You'll be made bring Deformed forth, I warrant you.

CONRADE Masters —

FIRST WATCHMAN Never speak, we charge you. Let us obey you to go with us.

BORACHIO We are like to prove a goodly commodity, being taken up of these men's bills.

CONRADE A commodity in question, I warrant you. Come, we'll obey you.

Exeunt

Act 3, Scene 4 — Hero Prepares for the Wedding

Margaret helps Hero get <u>ready</u> for the <u>wedding</u>. Beatrice says that she's feeling <u>ill</u> and Margaret <u>teases</u> her for being in <u>love</u>.

Photograph by Alastair Muir

ACT 3, SCENE 4

HERO'S APARTMENT

Enter HERO, MARGARET *and* URSULA

HERO	Good Ursula, wake my cousin Beatrice, and desire her to rise.	
URSULA	I will, lady.	
HERO	And bid her come hither.	
URSULA	Well.	5

Exit

MARGARET	Troth, I think your other rebato were better.	
HERO	No, pray thee, good Meg, I'll wear this.	
MARGARET	By my troth, 's not so good, and I warrant your cousin will say so.	
HERO	My cousin's a fool, and thou art another: I'll wear none but this.	10
MARGARET	I like the new tire within excellently, if the hair were a thought browner; and your gown's a most rare fashion, i' faith. I saw the Duchess of Milan's gown that they praise so.	15
HERO	O, that exceeds, they say.	
MARGARET	By my troth, 's but a night-gown in respect of yours: cloth o' gold, and cuts, and laced with silver, set with pearls, down sleeves, side sleeves and skirts, round underborne with a bluish tinsel; but for a fine, quaint, graceful and excellent fashion, yours is worth ten on 't.	20
HERO	God give me joy to wear it, for my heart is exceeding heavy.	
MARGARET	'Twill be heavier soon by the weight of a man.	25
HERO	Fie upon thee! Art not ashamed?	
MARGARET	Of what, lady? Of speaking honourably? Is not marriage honourable in a beggar? Is not your lord honourable without marriage? I think you would have me say, saving your reverence, 'a husband'. And bad thinking do not wrest true speaking, I'll offend nobody. Is there any harm in 'the heavier for a husband'? None, I think, and it be the right husband and the right wife, otherwise 'tis light, and not heavy. Ask my Lady Beatrice else — here she comes.	30 35

Enter BEATRICE

HERO	Good morrow, coz.

Shakespeare's Techniques

<u>Dramatic irony</u> creates a sense of <u>foreboding</u> in this scene — the <u>audience</u> knows that Hero is getting ready for a <u>wedding</u> that <u>isn't</u> going to <u>happen</u>.

6 A 'rebato' is a ruff (a piece of clothing worn round the neck, which was fashionable in Elizabethan times).

12 A 'tire' is a headdress.
12 'hair' means 'hair extensions attached to the ruff'.

17 'in respect of' means 'compared to'.

20 'the skirts are trimmed with blue tinsel material'.

23-24 A heavy heart was supposed to be a sign that something bad was about to happen.

Character — Margaret

Margaret is a <u>servant</u>, so it is more <u>acceptable</u> for her to talk about <u>sex</u> and make <u>bawdy jokes</u>. A <u>noblewoman</u> like Hero is meant to be '<u>pure</u>'.

29-32 'I think you would rather I said, to sound more respectful, 'a husband'. If bad thoughts do not twist the meaning of true words, I'll offend nobody.'

Act Three

Act 3, Scene 4

39 'Are you feeling out of sorts?'

41-42 'Let's sing 'Light of love' — that doesn't have a burden (a deep part for male voices)'.

43 'It's you who's light of love'.

43 'light-heeled' was a way of describing a woman who would sleep with anyone.

45 'barns' can also mean 'children'.

46-47 'That's really twisting the words! I'm walking away.'

Character — Beatrice

Beatrice seems <u>different</u> — she says she's <u>ill</u>, but really she's in <u>love</u>. This <u>mirrors</u> Benedick's '<u>toothache</u>' in Act 3, Scene 2.

52-53 'I'm as sure you've changed as sailors are sure of the North Star.'

54 'trow' means 'do you think'.

Shakespeare's Techniques

Beatrice says she has a <u>blocked nose</u>, but Margaret makes a <u>pun</u> and uses "<u>stuffed</u>" to mean '<u>pregnant</u>'.

62-63 'When did you start claiming to be quick on the uptake?'

64-65 'Ever since you stopped. Doesn't my wit suit me?'

68-69 'Carduus Benedictus' is a holy thistle used as a medicine. 'Benedictus' sounds like 'Benedick'.

70 'a qualm' means 'feeling sick'.

72-73 'You're trying to make a point with this Benedictus.'

76-81 'No, I'm not such a fool as to let myself believe what I want to believe, nor do I want to believe what I can believe, nor can I believe, even if I prevent my heart from thinking, that you are in love or will be in love or can be in love.'

84 'has a good appetite for love'.

BEATRICE	Good morrow, sweet Hero.	
HERO	Why how now? Do you speak in the sick tune?	
BEATRICE	I am out of all other tune, methinks.	40
MARGARET	Clap's into 'Light o' love' — that goes without a burden. Do you sing it, and I'll dance it.	
BEATRICE	Ye light o' love, with your heels! Then, if your husband have stables enough, you'll see he shall lack no barns.	45
MARGARET	O illegitimate construction! I scorn that with my heels.	
BEATRICE	'Tis almost five o'clock, cousin. 'Tis time you were ready. By my troth, I am exceeding ill. Heigh-ho!	
MARGARET	For a hawk, a horse, or a husband?	50
BEATRICE	For the letter that begins them all, H.	
MARGARET	Well, and you be not turned Turk, there's no more sailing by the star.	
BEATRICE	What means the fool, trow?	
MARGARET	Nothing I — but God send every one their heart's desire!	55
HERO	These gloves the count sent me — they are an excellent perfume.	
BEATRICE	I am stuffed, cousin. I cannot smell.	
MARGARET	A maid, and stuffed! There's goodly catching of cold.	60
BEATRICE	O, God help me! God help me! How long have you professed apprehension?	
MARGARET	Ever since you left it. Doth not my wit become me rarely?	65
BEATRICE	It is not seen enough, you should wear it in your cap. By my troth, I am sick.	
MARGARET	Get you some of this distilled Carduus Benedictus, and lay it to your heart — it is the only thing for a qualm.	70
HERO	There thou prickest her with a thistle.	
BEATRICE	Benedictus! Why Benedictus? You have some moral in this Benedictus.	
MARGARET	Moral! No, by my troth, I have no moral meaning; I meant, plain holy thistle. You may think perchance that I think you are in love. Nay, by'r lady, I am not such a fool to think what I list, nor I list not to think what I can, nor indeed I cannot think, if I would think my heart out of thinking, that you are in love or that you will be in love or that you can be in love. Yet Benedick was such another, and now is he become a man: he swore he would never marry, and yet now, in despite of his heart, he eats his meat without grudging:	75
		80

Act 3, Scene 5 — Dogberry Talks to Leonato

	and how you may be converted I know not, but methinks you look with your eyes as other women do.	85
BEATRICE	What pace is this that thy tongue keeps?	
MARGARET	Not a false gallop.	

Re-enter URSULA

| URSULA | Madam, withdraw — the prince, the count, Signior Benedick, Don John, and all the gallants of the town, are come to fetch you to church. | 90 |
| HERO | Help to dress me, good coz, good Meg, good Ursula. | |

Exeunt

88 'Why are you rattling on like this?'

90 'withdraw' means 'leave the room'.

91 'gallants' means 'gentlemen'.

Shakespeare's Techniques

Ursula's list emphasises that there will be lots of people at the wedding when Hero is shamed — this increases the tension.

Dogberry and Verges try to tell Leonato that they have arrested Borachio and Conrade, but they take too long to explain. Leonato is in a hurry to get to the wedding and leaves without hearing what they have to say.

ACT 3, SCENE 5

ANOTHER ROOM IN LEONATO'S HOUSE

Enter LEONATO, *with* DOGBERRY *and* VERGES

LEONATO	What would you with me, honest neighbour?	
DOGBERRY	Marry, sir, I would have some confidence with you that decerns you nearly.	
LEONATO	Brief, I pray you, for you see it is a busy time with me.	5
DOGBERRY	Marry, this it is, sir.	
VERGES	Yes, in truth it is, sir.	
LEONATO	What is it, my good friends?	
DOGBERRY	Goodman Verges, sir, speaks a little off the matter: an old man, sir, and his wits are not so blunt as, God help, I would desire they were, but, in faith, honest as the skin between his brows.	10
VERGES	Yes, I thank God I am as honest as any man living that is an old man and no honester than I.	
DOGBERRY	Comparisons are odorous: palabras, neighbour Verges.	15
LEONATO	Neighbours, you are tedious.	
DOGBERRY	It pleases your worship to say so, but we are the poor duke's officers. But truly, for mine own part, if I were as tedious as a king, I could find in my heart to bestow it all of your worship.	20
LEONATO	All thy tediousness on me, ah?	

2 'some confidence' means 'a word in private'.

3 He means 'concerns'.

Character — Leonato

Leonato is polite at first, but grows more frustrated with Dogberry and Verges. He becomes sarcastic (line 40) and impatient (line 42).

9-10 'wanders off the point a bit'.

Shakespeare's Techniques

Dogberry babbles rather than telling Leonato what he knows about Borachio. This creates tension for the audience.

15 'odorous' means 'smelly'. He means 'odious' (hateful).

15 'palabras' is Dogberry's version of the Spanish phrase 'pocas palabras' ('a few words'). He's telling Verges not to talk so much.

20-21 'I would find it in my heart to give all my tediousness to you.'

Act Three

48

Act 3, Scene 5

an means 'if'.

24-25 'I hear as good
things said about you as
about any man in the city'.

28 'I'd love to know what
it is you're going to tell me.'

31 'arrant knaves' means
'complete villains'.

Character — Dogberry

Dogberry is <u>self-important</u>
— he thinks that he is
<u>better</u> than Verges. This is
<u>humorous</u> — the audience
can see how <u>useless</u> he is.

40 'he doesn't match
your standards.'

44 He means 'suspicious'.
'auspicious' means 'favourable'.

49 He means 'sufficient'.

51 'stay' means 'wait'.

Shakespeare's Techniques

This is <u>frustrating</u> for the
audience — Leonato
leaves for the <u>wedding</u>
without finding out about
the <u>plot</u> against Hero. This
is a <u>missed opportunity</u>
for the <u>truth</u> to come out.

58-59 'non-come' is another
mistake from Dogberry. He
means 'We'll drive some of
them into a state of confusion'.

61 He means 'communication'.

DOGBERRY	Yea, an 'twere a thousand pound more than 'tis; for I hear as good exclamation on your worship as of any man in the city and though I be but a poor man, I am glad to hear it.
VERGES	And so am I.
LEONATO	I would fain know what you have to say.
VERGES	Marry, sir, our Watch tonight, excepting your worship's presence, ha' ta'en a couple of as arrant knaves as any in Messina.
DOGBERRY	A good old man, sir. He will be talking — as they say 'when the age is in, the wit is out'. God help us, it is a world to see! Well said, i' faith, neighbour Verges. Well, God's a good man; an two men ride of a horse, one must ride behind. An honest soul, i' faith, sir; by my troth he is, as ever broke bread; but God is to be worshipped — all men are not alike, alas, good neighbour!
LEONATO	Indeed, neighbour, he comes too short of you.
DOGBERRY	Gifts that God gives.
LEONATO	I must leave you.
DOGBERRY	One word, sir: our Watch, sir, have indeed comprehended two aspicious persons, and we would have them this morning examined before your worship.
LEONATO	Take their examination yourself and bring it me: I am now in great haste, as it may appear unto you.
DOGBERRY	It shall be suffigance.
LEONATO	Drink some wine ere you go. Fare you well!

Enter a Messenger

MESSENGER	My lord, they stay for you to give your daughter to her husband.
LEONATO	I'll wait upon them: I am ready.

Exeunt LEONATO and Messenger

DOGBERRY	Go, good partner, go, get you to Francis Seacole — bid him bring his pen and inkhorn to the gaol: we are now to examination these men.
VERGES	And we must do it wisely.
DOGBERRY	We will spare for no wit, I warrant you. Here's that shall drive some of them to a non-come: only get the learned writer to set down our excommunication and meet me at the gaol.

Exeunt

25, 30, 35, 40, 45, 50, 55, 60

Act Three

Act Three — Practice Questions

Quick Questions

1) Which two characters help Hero to trick Beatrice?

2) Give two examples of how Hero criticises Beatrice in Act 3, Scene 1.

3) How does Beatrice react to the news that Benedick is in love with her?

4) What does Benedick give as an excuse for his serious mood in Act 3, Scene 2?

5) What do Claudio and Don Pedro say they will do if they find out Hero has been unfaithful?

6) What was the role of the Watch in Elizabethan England?

7) How much did Don John pay Borachio for helping to deceive Claudio?

8) According to Borachio, how did Claudio react to what he saw at Hero's window?

9) Who teases Beatrice about being in love?

10) Why is Leonato in a hurry in Act 3, Scene 5?

In-depth Questions

1) Why do you think that Shakespeare wrote Act 3, Scene 1 in verse?

2) Describe the similarities between Beatrice being tricked in Act 3, Scene 1 and Benedick being tricked in Act 2, Scene 3. Why do you think Shakespeare chose to do this?

3) How does Beatrice behave differently in Act 3 compared to in Acts 1 and 2?

4) Why do you think Hero speaks more freely when there are no men around?

5) How does Shakespeare show the importance of honour in Act 3, Scene 2?

6) Explain how Shakespeare uses Dogberry and his language to create humour.

7) How does Shakespeare create and build tension throughout Act 3?

8) Imagine you are a costume designer for a production of *Much Ado About Nothing*. Describe the sort of clothes you would give Dogberry and Verges, and explain your choices.

Act 4, Scene 1 — Hero is Rejected at the Wedding

© Geraint Lewis / Alamy Stock Photo

Everyone gathers at the <u>church</u> for Claudio and Hero's <u>wedding</u>. Claudio announces he <u>won't marry</u> Hero and <u>accuses</u> her of being <u>unfaithful</u>. The <u>Friar</u> comes up with a plan to prove her <u>innocence</u>. Afterwards, Benedick and Beatrice admit their <u>love</u> to each other.

ACT 4, SCENE 1

A CHURCH

Enter DON PEDRO, DON JOHN, LEONATO, FRIAR FRANCIS, CLAUDIO, BENEDICK, HERO, BEATRICE *and Attendants*

1-3 'Just do the simple version of the service, and give them the lecture on how they should behave afterwards.'

LEONATO	Come, Friar Francis, be brief. Only to the plain form of marriage, and you shall recount their particular duties afterwards.	
FRIAR FRANCIS	You come hither, my lord, to marry this lady?	
CLAUDIO	No.	5
LEONATO	To be married to her. Friar, you come to marry her.	
FRIAR FRANCIS	Lady, you come hither to be married to this count?	
HERO	I do.	

10-12 'If either of you know of any reason why you should not be married, I order you to reveal it now.'

FRIAR FRANCIS	If either of you know any inward impediment why you should not be conjoined, I charge you, on your souls, to utter it.	10
CLAUDIO	Know you any, Hero?	
HERO	None, my lord.	
FRIAR FRANCIS	Know you any, count?	15
LEONATO	I dare make his answer — none.	
CLAUDIO	O, what men dare do! What men may do! What men daily do, not knowing what they do!	

Shakespeare's Techniques

The scene starts in <u>prose</u>, but Claudio switches to <u>verse</u>. This makes the scene more <u>dramatic</u> and <u>serious</u>.

19-20 Benedick tries to make a joke of Claudio's interruption.

BENEDICK	How now! Interjections? Why, then, some be of laughing, as, ah, ha, he!	20

22 'a clear conscience'.

26 'counterpoise' means 'balance'.

27 'render her again' means 'give her back again'.

28 'you have taught me to be truly grateful.'

CLAUDIO	Stand thee by, friar. Father, by your leave, Will you with free and unconstrained soul Give me this maid, your daughter?	
LEONATO	As freely, son, as God did give her me.	
CLAUDIO	And what have I to give you back, whose worth May counterpoise this rich and precious gift?	25
DON PEDRO	Nothing, unless you render her again.	

Shakespeare's Techniques

Through this <u>metaphor</u>, Claudio implies that Hero is <u>beautiful</u> on the <u>outside</u> but <u>rotten</u> on the <u>inside</u>.

CLAUDIO	Sweet Prince, you learn me noble thankfulness. There, Leonato, take her back again: Give not this rotten orange to your friend — She's but the sign and semblance of her honour. Behold how like a maid she blushes here! O, what authority and show of truth Can cunning sin cover itself withal! Comes not that blood as modest evidence To witness simple virtue? Would you not swear, All you that see her, that she were a maid,	30
		35

31-36 'She only has the appearance of honour. Look, she's blushing like a virgin! Cunning sin disguises itself so convincingly! Isn't blushing supposed to be proof of innocence?'

Act 4, Scene 1

	By these exterior shows? But she is none:	
	She knows the heat of a luxurious bed,	
	Her blush is guiltiness, not modesty.	40
LEONATO	What do you mean, my lord?	
CLAUDIO	Not to be married, not to knit my soul	
	To an approved wanton.	
LEONATO	Dear my lord, if you, in your own proof,	
	Have vanquished the resistance of her youth,	45
	And made defeat of her virginity —	
CLAUDIO	I know what you would say. If I have known her,	
	You will say she did embrace me as a husband,	
	And so extenuate the forehand sin.	
	No, Leonato.	50
	I never tempted her with word too large,	
	But, as a brother to his sister, showed	
	Bashful sincerity and comely love.	
HERO	And seemed I ever otherwise to you?	
CLAUDIO	Out on thee, seeming! I will write against it.	55
	You seem to me as Dian in her orb,	
	As chaste as is the bud ere it be blown;	
	But you are more intemperate in your blood	
	Than Venus, or those pampered animals	
	That rage in savage sensuality.	60
HERO	Is my lord well, that he doth speak so wide?	
LEONATO	Sweet Prince, why speak not you?	
DON PEDRO	What should I speak?	
	I stand dishonoured, that have gone about	
	To link my dear friend to a common stale.	
LEONATO	Are these things spoken, or do I but dream?	65
DON JOHN	Sir, they are spoken, and these things are true.	
BENEDICK	This looks not like a nuptial.	
HERO	True! O God!	
CLAUDIO	Leonato, stand I here?	
	Is this the Prince? Is this the Prince's brother?	
	Is this face Hero's? Are our eyes our own?	70
LEONATO	All this is so: but what of this, my lord?	
CLAUDIO	Let me but move one question to your daughter,	
	And, by that fatherly and kindly power	
	That you have in her, bid her answer truly.	
LEONATO	I charge thee do so, as thou art my child.	75
HERO	O, God defend me! How am I beset!	
	What kind of catechising call you this?	
CLAUDIO	To make you answer truly to your name.	
HERO	Is it not Hero? Who can blot that name	
	With any just reproach?	
CLAUDIO	Marry, that can Hero;	80
	Hero itself can blot out Hero's virtue.	

39 Claudio is accusing Hero of having slept with men before.

43 'approved wanton' means 'sexually promiscuous woman'.

44-46 'if you yourself have taken her virginity —'

47-49 'If I have slept with her, you'll say she only did it because I was going to be her husband, so it's not really a sin.'

Theme — Deception and Misunderstanding

Claudio is angry because he thinks Hero isn't as pure as she "seemed". This is ironic — she is exactly as innocent as she seemed.

55 'Here's my argument.'

56-59 In Roman mythology, Diana was the virgin goddess of hunting and the moon. Venus was the goddess of love and sex.

58 'intemperate' means 'without self-control'.

61 'Are you ill, speaking like this?'

64 'common stale' means 'disgraced woman'.

67 'nuptial' means 'wedding'.

Character — Hero

As a quiet and obedient Elizabethan woman, Hero feels powerless to defend herself as the men harshly accuse her.

76 'Everyone's turned on me!'

77 'catechising' means 'interrogation'.

79-80 'Who can harm my reputation with any truthful accusation?'

Act 4, Scene 1

	What man was he talked with you yesternight	
	Out at your window betwixt twelve and one?	
	Now, if you are a maid, answer to this.	
HERO	I talked with no man at that hour, my lord.	85
DON PEDRO	Why, then are you no maiden. Leonato,	
	I am sorry you must hear — upon mine honour,	
	Myself, my brother and this grieved count	
	Did see her, hear her, at that hour last night	
	Talk with a ruffian at her chamber-window,	90
	Who hath indeed, most like a liberal villain,	
	Confessed the vile encounters they have had	
	A thousand times in secret.	
DON JOHN	Fie, fie, they are not to be named, my lord,	
	Not to be spoke of!	95
	There is not chastity enough in language	
	Without offence to utter them. Thus, pretty lady,	
	I am sorry for thy much misgovernment.	
CLAUDIO	O Hero, what a Hero hadst thou been,	
	If half thy outward graces had been placed	100
	About thy thoughts and counsels of thy heart!	
	But fare thee well, most foul, most fair! Farewell,	
	Thou pure impiety and impious purity!	
	For thee I'll lock up all the gates of love,	
	And on my eyelids shall conjecture hang,	105
	To turn all beauty into thoughts of harm,	
	And never shall it more be gracious.	
LEONATO	Hath no man's dagger here a point for me?	
	HERO swoons	
BEATRICE	Why, how now, cousin! Wherefore sink you down?	
DON JOHN	Come, let us go. These things, come thus to light,	110
	Smother her spirits up.	
	Exeunt DON PEDRO, DON JOHN *and* CLAUDIO	
BENEDICK	How doth the lady?	
BEATRICE	Dead, I think. Help, uncle!	
	Hero! Why, Hero! Uncle! Signior Benedick! Friar!	
LEONATO	O Fate! Take not away thy heavy hand.	
	Death is the fairest cover for her shame	115
	That may be wished for.	
BEATRICE	How now, cousin Hero!	
FRIAR FRANCIS	Have comfort, lady.	
LEONATO	Dost thou look up?	
FRIAR FRANCIS	Yea, wherefore should she not?	
LEONATO	Wherefore! Why, doth not every earthly thing	
	Cry shame upon her? Could she here deny	120
	The story that is printed in her blood?	
	Do not live, Hero, do not ope thine eyes,	
	For, did I think thou wouldst not quickly die,	
	Thought I thy spirits were stronger than thy shames,	

Theme — Honour and Reputation

Don Pedro has a higher social status than the other characters, which means they believe his accusations. This is ironic — the audience knows that he's been deceived and that Hero is telling the truth.

96-98 'There isn't pure enough language to describe it without causing offence. I'm sorry, pretty lady, that you've behaved so badly.'

99-101 'Oh Hero, what a Hero you would have been, if your behaviour was half as good as your appearance!' In Greek mythology, Hero was a virgin priestess.

104-105 'Because of you, I'll close my heart, and make myself suspicious of everything I see.'

Stagecraft

This moment would look very dramatic on stage ("swoons" means 'faints'). It shows the audience the impact of the slander and creates sympathy for Hero.

109 'Wherefore' means 'why'.

Theme — Deception and Misunderstanding

Leonato thinks that Hero blushing is proof of her guilt (like Claudio did in lines 32-36), but really it is a sign of her innocence.

Act 4, Scene 1

Myself would, on the rearward of reproaches, 125
Strike at thy life. Grieved I, I had but one?
Chid I for that at frugal nature's frame?
O, one too much by thee! Why had I one?
Why ever wast thou lovely in my eyes?
Why had I not with charitable hand 130
Took up a beggar's issue at my gates,
Who smirched thus and mired with infamy,
I might have said 'No part of it is mine —
This shame derives itself from unknown loins'?
But mine and mine I loved and mine I praised 135
And mine that I was proud on, mine so much
That I myself was to myself not mine,
Valuing of her — why, she, O, she is fallen
Into a pit of ink, that the wide sea
Hath drops too few to wash her clean again, 140
And salt too little which may season give
To her foul-tainted flesh!

BENEDICK   Sir, sir, be patient.
For my part, I am so attired in wonder,
I know not what to say.

BEATRICE   O, on my soul, my cousin is belied! 145

BENEDICK   Lady, were you her bedfellow last night?

BEATRICE   No, truly not, although, until last night,
I have this twelvemonth been her bedfellow.

LEONATO   Confirmed, confirmed! O, that is stronger made
Which was before barred up with ribs of iron! 150
Would the two princes lie, and Claudio lie,
Who loved her so, that, speaking of her foulness,
Washed it with tears? Hence from her! Let her die.

FRIAR FRANCIS   Hear me a little;
For I have only been silent so long, 155
And given way unto this course of fortune,
By noting of the lady. I have marked
A thousand blushing apparitions
To start into her face, a thousand innocent shames
In angel whiteness beat away those blushes, 160
And in her eye there hath appeared a fire,
To burn the errors that these princes hold
Against her maiden truth. Call me a fool;
Trust not my reading nor my observations,
Which with experimental seal doth warrant 165
The tenor of my book; trust not my age,
My reverence, calling, nor divinity,
If this sweet lady lie not guiltless here
Under some biting error.

LEONATO   Friar, it cannot be.
Thou seest that all the grace that she hath left 170
Is that she will not add to her damnation
A sin of perjury: she not denies it.

123-128 'If I thought you weren't going to die, or that your will to live was stronger than your shame, then in my anger I would kill you myself. Was I upset that I had only one child? Did I complain at nature for not being more generous? Oh, you are one child too many!'

131 'issue' means 'child'.

133-134 'Then I could have blamed an unknown father for this shame'.

Theme — Honour and Reputation

Leonato's metaphor suggests Hero is stained by the accusations and her reputation is ruined forever.

143 'attired in wonder' means 'amazed'.

145 'belied' means 'falsely accused'.

Shakespeare's Techniques

This imagery of metal shows how strong Leonato believes the men's accusations are. Beatrice saying she didn't sleep in Hero's room makes him even more certain.

155-157 'I've only been quiet this long and let events run their course because I was observing Hero.'

Character — Friar Francis

The Friar is calm and rational. He isn't misled by Hero blushing — he knows it's a sign of her innocence.

164-166 'Don't trust my judgement of the situation, which is backed up by my great experience and knowledge'. The Friar thinks Hero is innocent and he's willing to stake his reputation on it.

167 'calling' means 'profession'.

170-172 'The only thing in her favour is that she doesn't add to her sins by trying to deny it.'

Act Four

Act 4, Scene 1

173-174 'So why are you trying to cover up the clear truth with excuses?'

Why seek'st thou then to cover with excuse
That which appears in proper nakedness?

FRIAR FRANCIS   Lady, what man is he you are accused of?   175

HERO   They know that do accuse me; I know none.
If I know more of any man alive
Than that which maiden modesty doth warrant,
Let all my sins lack mercy! O my father,
Prove you that any man with me conversed   180
At hours unmeet, or that I yesternight
Maintained the change of words with any creature,
Refuse me, hate me, torture me to death!

177-179 'If I know more about any man alive than a modest virgin should, then let me be damned!'

180-182 'Prove that any man spoke with me at an unsuitable hour, or that I spoke with anyone last night'.

184 'misprision' means 'misunderstanding'.

FRIAR FRANCIS   There is some strange misprision in the princes.

BENEDICK   Two of them have the very bent of honour,   185
And if their wisdoms be misled in this,
The practice of it lives in John the bastard,
Whose spirits toil in frame of villainies.

Character — Leonato

Previously, Leonato has been <u>mature</u> and <u>dignified</u>, but in this scene he acts <u>rashly</u> and speaks <u>violently</u>.

LEONATO   I know not. If they speak but truth of her,
These hands shall tear her. If they wrong
                                        her honour,   190
The proudest of them shall well hear of it.
Time hath not yet so dried this blood of mine,
Nor age so eat up my invention,
Nor fortune made such havoc of my means,
Nor my bad life reft me so much of friends,   195
But they shall find, awaked in such a kind,
Both strength of limb and policy of mind,
Ability in means and choice of friends,
To quit me of them throughly.

193 'invention' means 'mental powers'.

194 'Nor has fortune so destroyed my wealth'.

195 'reft' means 'deprived'.

197 'policy of mind' means 'clear thinking'.

199 'To have my full revenge on them'.

FRIAR FRANCIS   Pause awhile,
And let my counsel sway you in this case.   200
Your daughter here the princes left for dead,
Let her awhile be secretly kept in,
And publish it that she is dead indeed;
Maintain a mourning ostentation
And on your family's old monument   205
Hang mournful epitaphs and do all rites
That appertain unto a burial.

Theme — Deception and Misunderstanding

The Friar suggests that they <u>pretend</u> Hero is <u>dead</u>. It's <u>ironic</u> that a <u>religious</u> figure is encouraging <u>deception</u> — this shows how <u>widespread</u> deception is in the play.

LEONATO   What shall become of this? What will this do?

FRIAR FRANCIS   Marry, this well carried shall on her behalf
Change slander to remorse — that is some good —   210
But not for that dream I on this strange course,
But on this travail look for greater birth.
She dying, as it must so be maintained,
Upon the instant that she was accused,
Shall be lamented, pitied and excused   215
Of every hearer: for it so falls out
That what we have we prize not to the worth
Whiles we enjoy it, but being lacked and lost,
Why, then we rack the value, then we find
The virtue that possession would not show us   220

209-212 'If this goes well, we'll change the accusations for sorrow — which is something — but that's not my main reason for coming up with this strange plan. I'm hoping for an even better result.'

217-221 'we don't value what we have while we have it — only when it's lost and gone do we see the goodness that we ignored. That's how it will be with Claudio.'

Act Four

Act 4, Scene 1

Whiles it was ours. So will it fare with Claudio.
When he shall hear she died upon his words,
The idea of her life shall sweetly creep
Into his study of imagination,
And every lovely organ of her life   225
Shall come apparelled in more precious habit,
More moving-delicate and full of life,
Into the eye and prospect of his soul,
Than when she lived indeed. Then shall he mourn,
If ever love had interest in his liver,   230
And wish he had not so accused her,
No, though he thought his accusation true.
Let this be so, and doubt not but success
Will fashion the event in better shape
Than I can lay it down in likelihood.   235
But if all aim but this be levelled false,
The supposition of the lady's death   *when people*
Will quench the wonder of her infamy.   *believe she is*
                                                 dead they will forget
And if it sort not well, you may conceal her,   *if it*
As best befits her wounded reputation,   *doesn't* 240
In some <u>reclusive and religious life</u>,   *work*
                                                 conceal her
Out of all eyes, tongues, minds and injuries.

BENEDICK   Signior Leonato, let the friar advise you,
                  And though you know my inwardness and love
                  Is very much unto the Prince and Claudio,   245
                  Yet, by mine honour, I will deal in this
                  As secretly and justly as your soul
                  Should with your body.

LEONATO   Being that I flow in grief,
                  The smallest twine may lead me.

FRIAR FRANCIS   'Tis well consented. Presently away;   250
                  For to strange sores strangely they strain the cure.
                  Come, lady, die to live. This wedding-day
                  Perhaps is but prolonged. Have patience and
                                                            endure.

                  Exeunt all but BENEDICK *and* BEATRICE

BENEDICK   Lady Beatrice, have you wept all this while?

BEATRICE   Yea, and I will weep a while longer.   255

BENEDICK   I will not desire that.

BEATRICE   You have no reason — I do it freely.

BENEDICK   Surely I do believe your fair cousin is wronged.

BEATRICE   Ah, how much might the man deserve of me that
                  would right her!   260

BENEDICK   Is there any way to show such friendship?

BEATRICE   A very even way, but no such friend.

BENEDICK   May a man do it?

BEATRICE   It is a man's office, but not yours.

BENEDICK   I do love nothing in the world so well as you: is 265
                  not that strange?

225-226 'And everything that was lovely about her in life will seem even more precious'.

229-230 'Then, if he has ever had true feelings of love, he will mourn'.

236-238 'But even if the whole plan comes to nothing, at least her supposed death will distract people from the scandal.'

Theme — Gender

If Hero <u>isn't</u> proved <u>innocent</u>, she will be sent to a <u>nunnery</u>. The Friar thinks that it's better for a <u>disgraced woman</u> to live <u>away</u> from <u>society</u>. Hero <u>doesn't</u> get a <u>say</u> in this.

248-249 'I'm so upset, I'll do whatever I'm told.'

251 'There are strange remedies for strange illnesses.'

Characters — Benedick and Beatrice

Benedick and Beatrice are left <u>alone</u> together on stage. She is <u>upset</u> and he <u>comforts</u> her — this is a very <u>different</u> situation for them and marks a <u>turning point</u> in their <u>relationship</u>.

262 'even' means 'straightforward'.

264 'office' means 'job'.

Act 4, Scene 1

Theme — Love and Marriage

Benedick and Beatrice admit their <u>love</u> for each other, but it is a <u>bittersweet</u> moment — Beatrice is still <u>devastated</u> about Hero.

273 'Don't swear to something and then take it back.'

281-282 'You've stopped me just at the right moment. I was about to announce that I loved you.'

Shakespeare's Techniques

Beatrice's response is a <u>short</u>, <u>sharp command</u> — it <u>shocks</u> both Benedick and the <u>audience</u>.

290 'Tarry' means 'wait'.

296-297 'You'd rather be my friend than fight my enemy.'

301-304 'He led her on right until the last minute, and then publicly accused her and bitterly told lies about her'.

Theme — Gender

Beatrice uses <u>harsh</u>, <u>violent</u> language. She feels <u>frustrated</u> that <u>men</u> can <u>slander</u> her cousin and she is <u>powerless</u> to do anything about it because she's a <u>woman</u>.

307 'What a ridiculous thing to say!'

BEATRICE	As strange as the thing I know not. It were as possible for me to say I loved nothing so well as you. But believe me not; and yet I lie not. I confess nothing, nor I deny nothing. I am sorry for my cousin.	270
BENEDICK	By my sword, Beatrice, thou lovest me.	
BEATRICE	Do not swear and eat it.	
BENEDICK	I will swear by it that you love me, and I will make him eat it that says I love not you.	275
BEATRICE	Will you not eat your word?	
BENEDICK	With no sauce that can be devised to it. I protest I love thee.	
BEATRICE	Why, then, God forgive me!	
BENEDICK	What offence, sweet Beatrice?	280
BEATRICE	You have stayed me in a happy hour. I was about to protest I loved you.	
BENEDICK	And do it with all thy heart.	
BEATRICE	I love you with so much of my heart that none is left to protest.	285
BENEDICK	Come, bid me do anything for thee.	
BEATRICE	<u>Kill Claudio</u>.	
BENEDICK	Ha! Not for the wide world.	
BEATRICE	You kill me to deny it. Farewell.	
BENEDICK	Tarry, sweet Beatrice.	290
BEATRICE	I am gone, though I am here. There is no love in you. Nay, I pray you, let me go.	
BENEDICK	Beatrice —	
BEATRICE	In faith, I will go.	
BENEDICK	We'll be friends first.	295
BEATRICE	You dare easier be friends with me than fight with mine enemy.	
BENEDICK	Is Claudio thine enemy?	
BEATRICE	Is a' not approved in the height a villain, that hath slandered, scorned, dishonoured my kinswoman? O that I were a man! What, bear her in hand until they come to take hands, and then, with public accusation, uncovered slander, unmitigated rancour — O God, that I were a man! I would eat his heart in the market-place.	300 / 305
BENEDICK	Hear me, Beatrice —	
BEATRICE	Talk with a man out at a window! A proper saying!	
BENEDICK	Nay, but, Beatrice —	
BEATRICE	Sweet Hero! She is wronged, she is slandered, she is undone.	310
BENEDICK	Beat —	
BEATRICE	Princes and counties! Surely, a princely	

Act 4, Scene 2 — Don John's Plot is Discovered

	testimony, a goodly count, Count Comfect, a sweet gallant, surely! O that I were a man for his sake! Or that I had any friend would be a man for my sake! But manhood is melted into curtsies, valour into compliment, and men are only turned into tongue, and trim ones too. He is now as valiant as Hercules that only tells a lie and swears it. I cannot be a man with wishing, therefore I will die a woman with grieving.	315
		320
BENEDICK	Tarry, good Beatrice. By this hand, I love thee.	
BEATRICE	Use it for my love some other way than swearing by it.	
BENEDICK	Think you in your soul the Count Claudio hath wronged Hero?	325
BEATRICE	Yea, as sure as I have a thought or a soul.	
BENEDICK	Enough, I am engaged. I will challenge him. I will kiss your hand, and so I leave you. By this hand, Claudio shall render me a dear account. As you hear of me, so think of me. Go, comfort your cousin. I must say she is dead, and so, farewell.	330

Exeunt

313 'Count Sugarplum'. Beatrice is mocking Claudio.

316-320 'Manhood has been watered down into politeness, bravery into flattery, and men are nothing but measly words. A man who tells a lie and swears it's true is now considered as brave as Hercules.'

Theme — Loyalty

Beatrice is loyal to Hero from the moment she is accused. She challenges Benedick's loyalty to Claudio — he eventually agrees to duel Claudio to prove his love for Beatrice.

328 'engaged' means 'committed'.

329-330 'I swear, Claudio will pay dearly for what he has done.'

Dogberry, Verges and the Sexton interrogate Borachio and Conrade, and Don John's plot is discovered.

ACT 4, SCENE 2

Photo by Reg Wilson © RSC.

A PRISON

Enter DOGBERRY, VERGES and SEXTON in gowns, and the Watch, with CONRADE and BORACHIO

DOGBERRY	Is our whole dissembly appeared?	
VERGES	O, a stool and a cushion for the Sexton.	
SEXTON	Which be the malefactors?	
DOGBERRY	Marry, that am I and my partner.	
VERGES	Nay, that's certain. We have the exhibition to examine.	5
SEXTON	But which are the offenders that are to be examined? Let them come before master constable.	
DOGBERRY	Yea, marry, let them come before me. What is your name, friend?	10
BORACHIO	Borachio.	

1 He means 'assembly'.

2 A 'sexton' is a church official.

3 'malefactors' means 'criminals'.

Shakespeare's Techniques

Dogberry says that he and Verges are the criminals. His incompetence provides comedy and lightens the mood after the tragic events of the previous scene.

Act 4, Scene 2

13 'sirrah' means 'boy'.

DOGBERRY	Pray, write down, Borachio. Yours, sirrah?	
CONRADE	I am a gentleman, sir, and my name is Conrade.	
DOGBERRY	Write down, master gentleman Conrade. Masters, do you serve God?	15
CONRADE *and* BORACHIO	Yea, sir, we hope.	

19-20 'write God first, for God must go before rascals like these!'

21-22 'and soon we'll almost know for sure'.

| DOGBERRY | Write down, that they hope they serve God, and write God first, for God defend but God should go before such villains! Masters, it is proved already that you are little better than false knaves, and it will go near to be thought so shortly. How answer you for yourselves? | 20 |
| CONRADE | Marry, sir, we say we are none. | |

26 'get the better of him'.

30-31 'By God, it looks as though they've got their story straight. Have you written down that they're not lying criminals?'

32 'you're not questioning them right.'

DOGBERRY	A marvellous witty fellow, I assure you, but I will go about with him. Come you hither, sirrah. A word in your ear. Sir, I say to you, it is thought you are false knaves.	25
BORACHIO	Sir, I say to you we are none.	
DOGBERRY	Well, stand aside. 'Fore God, they are both in a tale. Have you writ down that they are none?	30

Character — The Sexton

The Sexton is a plot device — Shakespeare uses him to make sure that the truth about Don John's plan is discovered.

| SEXTON | Master constable, you go not the way to examine. You must call forth the Watch that are their accusers. | |

35 He probably means 'best'.

| DOGBERRY | Yea, marry, that's the eftest way. Let the Watch come forth. Masters, I charge you, in the Prince's name, accuse these men. | 35 |
| FIRST WATCHMAN | This man said, sir, that Don John, the Prince's brother, was a villain. | |

Theme — Deception and Misunderstanding

Dogberry misunderstands what Borachio and Conrade's crimes are. It is ironic that he is credited with discovering the truth.

DOGBERRY	Write down, Prince John a villain. Why, this is flat perjury, to call a Prince's brother villain.	40
BORACHIO	Master constable —	
DOGBERRY	Pray thee, fellow, peace. I do not like thy look, I promise thee.	
SEXTON	What heard you him say else?	45
SECOND WATCHMAN	Marry, that he had received a thousand ducats of Don John for accusing the Lady Hero wrongfully.	
DOGBERRY	Flat burglary as ever was committed.	
VERGES	Yea, by mass, that it is.	50
SEXTON	What else, fellow?	
FIRST WATCHMAN	And that Count Claudio did mean, upon his words, to disgrace Hero before the whole assembly, and not marry her.	

56 He means 'damnation'.

DOGBERRY	O villain! Thou wilt be condemned into everlasting redemption for this.	55
SEXTON	What else?	
WATCHMAN	This is all.	
SEXTON	And this is more, masters, than you can deny.	

Act 4, Scene 2

Prince John is this morning secretly stolen 60
away. Hero was in this manner accused, in this
very manner refused, and upon the grief of this
suddenly died. Master constable, let these men
be bound, and brought to Leonato's. I will go
before and show him their examination. 65

Exit

DOGBERRY   Come, let them be opinioned.

VERGES   Let them be in the hands —

CONRADE   Off, coxcomb!

DOGBERRY   God's my life, where's the sexton? Let him write
down, the Prince's officer coxcomb. Come, bind 70
them. Thou naughty varlet!

CONRADE   Away! You are an ass, you are an ass. — *try and put him down*

DOGBERRY   Dost thou not suspect my place? Dost thou not
suspect my years? O that he were here to write
me down an ass! But, masters, remember that 75
I am an ass — though it be not written down,
yet forget not that I am an ass. No, thou villain,
thou art full of piety, as shall be proved upon
thee by good witness. I am a wise fellow, and,
which is more, an officer, and, which is more, 80
a householder, and, which is more, as pretty a
piece of flesh as any is in Messina, and one that
knows the law, go to; and a rich fellow enough, go
to; and a fellow that hath had losses, and one that
hath two gowns and everything handsome about 85
him. Bring him away. O that I had been writ
down an ass!

Exeunt

65 'their examination' means 'the results of the questioning'.

66 He means 'pinioned', which means 'restrained'.

68 A 'coxcomb' is the red crest on a cockerel's head. He's insulting Dogberry by calling him a fool.

71 'varlet' means 'scoundrel'.

73-74 He means 'respect'.

Theme — Honour and Reputation

Dogberry is <u>outraged</u> by Conrade's <u>insult</u>. <u>Honour</u> is an <u>important</u> issue for the <u>lower-status</u> characters as well as the <u>noble</u> ones.

Shakespeare's Techniques — Wordplay

Shakespeare uses <u>wordplay</u> to make Dogberry's <u>language humorous</u>. Many other characters provide humour because they are <u>witty</u>, but Dogberry is comic because of his <u>mistakes</u>. His speech is full of <u>malapropisms</u> — he uses a <u>wrong word</u> that <u>sounds like</u> the word he means (for example, he says '<u>suspect</u>' rather than '<u>respect</u>' in lines 73 and 74).

He is a <u>lower-status</u> character and tries to <u>copy</u> the <u>sophisticated</u> language of <u>noble</u> characters like Leonato to make himself sound <u>important</u>. However, he isn't <u>intelligent</u> enough to do this and usually ends up speaking <u>nonsense</u>.

© Donald Cooper / photostage

Act Four

Act Four — Practice Questions

Quick Questions

1) What is Claudio's 'proof' that Hero has been unfaithful?

2) Why does Leonato use a metaphor about ink to describe Hero?

3) Who suggests the plan to pretend Hero is dead?

4) Where might Hero be sent if she isn't proved innocent?

5) Why does Beatrice say that she wishes she were a man?

6) What does Benedick agree to do for Beatrice?

7) Who helps Dogberry and Verges interrogate the prisoners?

8) Find two examples of when Dogberry uses the wrong words in Act 4, Scene 2.

9) What makes Dogberry so angry with Conrade at the end of Act 4, Scene 2?

In-depth Questions

1) Do you think that Claudio loves Hero? Use examples from Act 4, Scene 1 in your answer.

2) Explain the importance of appearances in Act 4, Scene 1.

3) Give two examples of different phrases the men use to call Hero 'unfaithful' or 'disgraced'.
   What effect does this language have on the audience?

4) Do you think that Shakespeare presents Leonato as a good father? Explain your answer.

5) Explain how Shakespeare creates a serious atmosphere in Act 4, Scene 1.

6) How is Benedick and Beatrice's relationship presented in Act 4, Scene 1?
   Compare this to earlier scenes in the play.

7) Describe how Shakespeare shows that reputation is important to Dogberry in Act 4.

8) Imagine you are Hero. Write a diary entry about how you feel after the
   wedding and what you think about the plan to pretend that you're dead.

Act 5, Scene 1 — Don John's Plot is Revealed

Antonio and Leonato nearly <u>fight</u> Don Pedro and Claudio, then Benedick <u>challenges</u> Claudio to a <u>duel</u>. Dogberry arrives with Borachio and Conrade, and the <u>plot</u> to <u>ruin</u> Hero and Claudio's wedding is <u>revealed</u> at last.

Photo by Reg Wilson © RSC.

ACT 5, SCENE 1

BEFORE LEONATO'S HOUSE

Enter LEONATO *and* ANTONIO

ANTONIO	If you go on thus, you will kill yourself,	
	And 'tis not wisdom thus to second grief	
	Against yourself.	
LEONATO	I pray thee, cease thy counsel,	
	Which falls into mine ears as profitless	
	As water in a sieve. Give not me counsel,	5
	Nor let no comforter delight mine ear	
	But such a one whose wrongs do suit with mine.	
	Bring me a father that so loved his child,	
	Whose joy of her is overwhelmed like mine,	
	And bid him speak of patience;	10
	Measure his woe the length and breadth of mine	
	And let it answer every strain for strain,	
	As thus for thus and such a grief for such,	
	In every lineament, branch, shape, and form.	
	If such a one will smile and stroke his beard,	15
	Bid sorrow wag, cry 'hem!' when he should groan,	
	Patch grief with proverbs, make misfortune drunk	
	With candle-wasters; bring him yet to me,	
	And I of him will gather patience.	
	But there is no such man: for, brother, men	20
	Can counsel and speak comfort to that grief	
	Which they themselves not feel; but, tasting it,	
	Their counsel turns to passion, which before	
	Would give preceptial medicine to rage,	
	Fetter strong madness in a silken thread,	25
	Charm ache with air and agony with words.	
	No, no, 'tis all men's office to speak patience	
	To those that wring under the load of sorrow,	
	But no man's virtue nor sufficiency	
	To be so moral when he shall endure	30
	The like himself. Therefore give me no counsel.	
	My griefs cry louder than advertisement.	
ANTONIO	Therein do men from children nothing differ.	
LEONATO	I pray thee, peace. I will be flesh and blood;	
	For there was never yet philosopher	35
	That could endure the toothache patiently,	
	However they have writ the style of gods	
	And made a push at chance and sufferance.	
ANTONIO	Yet bend not all the harm upon yourself;	
	Make those that do offend you suffer too.	40

2-3 'it's not wise to turn your grief against yourself.'

Shakespeare's Techniques

Leonato speaks in <u>verse</u> and uses <u>dramatic</u>, <u>poetic language</u>. It's as though Hero is <u>really dead</u> and he's <u>grieving</u> for her.

11-12 'Compare that man's sadness against mine, and make sure he has been hurt just as much as I have'.

15-19 'If that man will smile and stroke his beard, tell me to ignore my sorrow, say 'Ahem!' when he should be groaning, offer proverbs as comfort for grief, drug my sorrow with second-rate philosophy — you can bring him to me, and I'll accept his advice to control myself.'

22-26 'but once they experience the problem personally, their advice turns to emotion, whereas before they'd think everything could be sorted out with words.'

27-31 'No, no, all men must advise those who suffer sorrow to be calm, but no man is so virtuous that he can go through the same himself.'

32 'advertisement' means 'advice'.

37-38 'However much his writings advised behaving in the manner of gods, and scoffed at misfortune and suffering.'

Act 5, Scene 1

LEONATO	There thou speak'st reason. Nay, I will do so. My soul doth tell me Hero is belied; And that shall Claudio know; so shall the Prince And all of them that thus dishonour her.
ANTONIO	Here comes the Prince and Claudio hastily.

45

Enter DON PEDRO and CLAUDIO

DON PEDRO	Good den, good den.
CLAUDIO	Good day to both of you.
LEONATO	Hear you, my lords —
DON PEDRO	We have some haste, Leonato.
LEONATO	Some haste, my lord! Well, fare you well, my lord! Are you so hasty now? Well, all is one.
DON PEDRO	Nay, do not quarrel with us, good old man.
ANTONIO	If he could right himself with quarrelling, Some of us would lie low.
CLAUDIO	Who wrongs him?
LEONATO	Marry, thou dost wrong me, thou dissembler, thou — Nay, never lay thy hand upon thy sword; I fear thee not.
CLAUDIO	Marry, beshrew my hand If it should give your age such cause of fear. In faith, my hand meant nothing to my sword.
LEONATO	Tush, tush, man, never fleer and jest at me! I speak not like a dotard nor a fool, As under privilege of age to brag What I have done being young, or what would do Were I not old. Know, Claudio, to thy head, Thou hast so wronged mine innocent child and me That I am forced to lay my reverence by And, with grey hairs and bruise of many days, Do challenge thee to trial of a man. I say thou hast belied mine innocent child. Thy slander hath gone through and through her heart, And she lies buried with her ancestors — O, in a tomb where never scandal slept, Save this of hers, framed by thy villainy!
CLAUDIO	My villainy?
LEONATO	Thine, Claudio; thine, I say.
DON PEDRO	You say not right, old man.
LEONATO	My lord, my lord, I'll prove it on his body, if he dare, Despite his nice fence and his active practice, His May of youth and bloom of lustihood.
CLAUDIO	Away! I will not have to do with you.
LEONATO	Canst thou so daff me? Thou hast killed my child. If thou kill'st me, boy, thou shalt kill a man.

50

55

60

65

70

75

42 'belied' means 'falsely accused'.

Character — Claudio

Claudio seems <u>foolish</u> as it should be <u>obvious</u> why Leonato is <u>angry</u> with him — as far as he knows, Hero is <u>dead</u>. His <u>insensitive</u> behaviour leads to the <u>confrontation</u>.

53 'dissembler' means 'liar'.

55-57 'Curse my hand, if it has frightened an old man like you. I promise you, I didn't mean anything by putting my hand on my sword.'

58 'fleer' means 'sneer'.

59-62 'I'm not speaking like a weak old man or a fool, who has an excuse to brag about what he did when he was young, or what he would do if he was not old.'

62 'I'm telling you to your face, Claudio'.

Character — Leonato

Leonato wants to get <u>revenge</u> for his "innocent child". He has <u>no chance</u> of <u>beating</u> Claudio in a <u>duel</u>, but he's so <u>angry</u> that he doesn't <u>care</u>.

74-76 'I'll prove it in a fight if he dares to take up the challenge, despite his fancy fencing skills, his training, his youth and his strength.'

78 'daff' means 'dismiss'.

Act 5, Scene 1

ANTONIO	He shall kill two of us, and men indeed.	80
	But that's no matter, let him kill one first.	
	Win me and wear me, let him answer me.	
	Come, follow me, boy. Come, sir boy, come,	
	follow me.	
	Sir boy, I'll whip you from your foining fence!	
	Nay, as I am a gentleman, I will.	85
LEONATO	Brother —	
ANTONIO	Content yourself. God knows I loved my niece,	
	And she is dead, slandered to death by villains,	
	That dare as well answer a man indeed	
	As I dare take a serpent by the tongue.	90
	Boys, apes, braggarts, Jacks, milksops!	
LEONATO	Brother Antony —	
ANTONIO	Hold you content. What, man! I know them, yea,	
	And what they weigh, even to the utmost scruple.	
	Scambling, out-facing, fashion-monging boys,	
	That lie and cog and flout, deprave and slander,	95
	Go anticly, show outward hideousness,	
	And speak off half a dozen dangerous words,	
	How they might hurt their enemies, if they durst —	
	And this is all.	
LEONATO	But, brother Antony —	
ANTONIO	Come, 'tis no matter.	100
	Do not you meddle; let me deal in this.	
DON PEDRO	Gentlemen both, we will not wake your patience.	
	My heart is sorry for your daughter's death,	
	But, on my honour, she was charged with nothing	
	But what was true and very full of proof.	105
LEONATO	My lord, my lord —	
DON PEDRO	I will not hear you.	
LEONATO	No? Come, brother; away! I will be heard.	
ANTONIO	And shall, or some of us will smart for it.	

Exeunt LEONATO *and* ANTONIO

| DON PEDRO | See, see! Here comes the man we went to seek. | 110 |

Enter BENEDICK

CLAUDIO	Now, signior, what news?	
BENEDICK	Good day, my lord.	
DON PEDRO	Welcome, signior. You are almost come to part almost a fray.	
CLAUDIO	We had like to have had our two noses snapped off with two old men without teeth.	115
DON PEDRO	Leonato and his brother. What thinkest thou? Had we fought, I doubt we should have been too young for them.	
BENEDICK	In a false quarrel there is no true valour. I came to seek you both.	120

82 'Beat me in a fight and I'm yours'.

84 'foining fence' is a style of sword-fighting where you block the other person's blows instead of trying to stab at them. Antonio's saying he wants a proper fight.

88-90 'her death caused by the lies of scoundrels who are as likely to fight a real man as I am to take a snake by the tongue.'

92-98 'You stay out of it! I know their sort, and just what they're like. Rough, competitive, fashion-crazy boys, who lie and cheat and mock, give others a bad name and behave wildly, babbling threats about how they'd hurt their enemies, if they dared'.

Theme — Loyalty

Antonio wants to support his brother and duel Claudio to defend their family's honour.

102 'we won't test your patience'.

Character — Don Pedro

Don Pedro doesn't seem genuinely sorry — he's just trying to avoid a fight. He still thinks that he and Claudio did the right thing.

109 'smart' means 'suffer'.

113-114 'You were almost in time to stop what was almost a fight.'

Theme — Honour and Reputation

Benedick is serious and has honourable intentions. In contrast, Claudio and Don Pedro's light-hearted behaviour is inappropriate.

Act Five

Act 5, Scene 1

122-123 'we are feeling sad'.	CLAUDIO	We have been up and down to seek thee, for we are high-proof melancholy and would fain have it beaten away. Wilt thou use thy wit?	
	BENEDICK	It is in my scabbard — shall I draw it?	125
	DON PEDRO	Dost thou wear thy wit by thy side?	
127-129 'Nobody has ever worn their wit by their side, though many have been beside themselves. I'm asking you to be funny like I'd ask a minstrel — to entertain us.'	CLAUDIO	Never any did so, though very many have been beside their wit. I will bid thee draw, as we do the minstrels — draw, to pleasure us.	
	DON PEDRO	As I am an honest man, he looks pale. Art thou sick, or angry?	130
132-133 'Sadness killed the cat, but you've got the guts to kill sadness.'	CLAUDIO	What, courage, man! What though care killed a cat, thou hast mettle enough in thee to kill care.	
134-135 'if you try to attack me with your wit, I'll meet you in the fight.' Benedick is using a jousting metaphor.	BENEDICK	Sir, I shall meet your wit in the career, and you charge it against me. I pray you choose another subject.	135
137-138 'Then give him another lance to fight with — the one he's got is broken.'	CLAUDIO	Nay, then, give him another staff; this last was broke cross.	
	DON PEDRO	By this light, he changes more and more. I think he be angry indeed.	140
141 'If he's angry, that's his problem.'	CLAUDIO	If he be, he knows how to turn his girdle.	
	BENEDICK	Shall I speak a word in your ear?	
143 'God bless me' means 'God save me'.	CLAUDIO	God bless me from a challenge!	
	BENEDICK	(Aside to Claudio) You are a villain. I jest not; I will make it good how you dare, with what you dare, and when you dare. Do me right, or I will protest your cowardice. You have killed a sweet lady, and her death shall fall heavy on you. Let me hear from you.	145

Theme — Honour and Reputation

Claudio has to <u>accept</u> Benedick's <u>challenge</u> or he'll be seen as a <u>coward</u> (see p.68).

	CLAUDIO	Well, I will meet you, so I may have good cheer.	150
	DON PEDRO	What, a feast, a feast?	
152-154 'I thank him — he's invited me to eat a calf's head and a chicken, and if I don't do an outstanding job of carving it, you can say my knife's useless.' Calves' heads and capons were associated with foolishness.	CLAUDIO	I' faith, I thank him, he hath bid me to a calf's head and a capon, the which if I do not carve most curiously, say my knife's naught. Shall I not find a woodcock too?	
155 A 'woodcock' is a bird known for being easy to catch.			155
	BENEDICK	Sir, your wit ambles well; it goes easily.	
161 'Just' means 'fair enough'.	DON PEDRO	I'll tell thee how Beatrice praised thy wit the other day. I said, thou hadst a fine wit: 'True,' said she, 'a fine little one.' 'No,' said I, 'a great wit.' 'Right,' says she, 'a great gross one.' 'Nay,' said I, 'a good wit.' 'Just,' said she, 'it hurts nobody.' 'Nay,' said I, 'the gentleman is wise.' 'Certain,' said she, 'a wise gentleman.' 'Nay,' said I, 'he hath the tongues.' 'That I believe,' said she, 'for he swore a thing to me on Monday night, which he forswore on Tuesday morning; there's a double tongue; there's two tongues.' Thus did she, an hour together, transshape thy particular virtues. Yet at last she concluded with a sigh, thou wast	160
163-167 "'No!' I said, 'he speaks several languages (tongues).' 'I can believe that,' she said, 'because he promised something to me on Monday night, and broke his promise on Tuesday morning — that's a double tongue for you''.			165
168 'transshape' means 'transform'.			

Act Five

Act 5, Scene 1

	the properest man in Italy.	170

170 'properest' means 'finest'.

CLAUDIO — For the which she wept heartily and said she cared not.

DON PEDRO — Yea, that she did: but yet, for all that, an if she did not hate him deadly, she would love him dearly — the old man's daughter told us all. **175**

CLAUDIO — All, all — and, moreover, God saw him when he was hid in the garden.

DON PEDRO — But when shall we set the savage bull's horns on the sensible Benedick's head?

Shakespeare's Techniques

Don Pedro jokes about Benedick being in love — he uses cuckold imagery, like Benedick did in Act 1, Scene 1 when he mocked marriage.

CLAUDIO — Yea, and text underneath, 'Here dwells Benedick the married man.' **180**

BENEDICK — Fare you well, boy, you know my mind. I will leave you now to your gossip-like humour. You break jests as braggarts do their blades, which God be thanked, hurt not. My lord, for your many courtesies I thank you. I must discontinue your company. Your brother the bastard is fled from Messina. You have among you killed a sweet and innocent lady. For my Lord Lackbeard there, he and I shall meet; and, till then, peace be with him. **185** **190**

Exit

183-185 'You make jokes, like bragging fools who break their swords — neither of them hurts a bit, thank God.'

Shakespeare's Techniques

Don John has fled, suggesting he's afraid his plot will be discovered. This hints that everything will soon be resolved.

DON PEDRO — He is in earnest.

CLAUDIO — In most profound earnest; and, I'll warrant you, for the love of Beatrice.

DON PEDRO — And hath challenged thee?

CLAUDIO — Most sincerely. **195**

189 Benedick's saying that Claudio is young and immature.

DON PEDRO — What a pretty thing man is when he goes in his doublet and hose and leaves off his wit!

CLAUDIO — He is then a giant to an ape, but then is an ape a doctor to such a man.

DON PEDRO — But, soft you, let me be! Pluck up, my heart, and be sad. Did he not say, my brother was fled? **200**

Enter DOGBERRY, VERGES *and the Watch,* *with* CONRADE *and* BORACHIO

DOGBERRY — Come you, sir. If justice cannot tame you, she shall ne'er weigh more reasons in her balance. Nay, an you be a cursing hypocrite once, you must be looked to. **205**

DON PEDRO — How now? Two of my brother's men bound! Borachio one!

CLAUDIO — Hearken after their offence, my lord.

DON PEDRO — Officers, what offence have these men done?

DOGBERRY — Marry, sir, they have committed false report. Moreover, they have spoken untruths; secondarily, they are slanders; sixth and lastly, they have belied a lady; thirdly, they have verified **210**

196-197 'Doesn't a man look ridiculous when he puts on his jacket and trousers and forgets his common sense!'

198-199 'A man who forgets his common sense is like a giant ape, but then an ape is as clever as a doctor compared to a man like that.'

200-201 'Shush a minute, let me think! It's time to stop messing around and be serious.'

202-205 'If justice can't sort you out, she'll give up altogether. Liars need to be dealt with.'

208 'Ask what they've done wrong'.

210-215 All different ways of saying, 'They've told lies.'

Act 5, Scene 1

216-219 All different ways of saying, 'What have they done?'

220-221 'Perfectly logical, in his own style, and, I swear, there's one meaning well disguised.'

Character — Don Pedro

Don Pedro mocks Dogberry and his confused speech. This is ironic, because Dogberry uncovered the trick that fooled Don Pedro.

226-227 'don't make me answer, just let Claudio kill me.'

232 'incensed' means 'incited' or 'encouraged'.

Shakespeare's Techniques

Shakespeare uses imagery of "iron" and "poison" to show Don Pedro and Claudio's horror that their actions led to Hero's death when she was innocent.

248-249 'Now I can see you as I did when I first loved you.'

250 He's using the wrong word — 'plaintiffs' are 'accusers'.

251 He means 'informed'.

252-253 'when the time and place are right, do not forget to make it clear that I am an ass.'

Shakespeare's Techniques

In this scene and the next one, the truth is revealed to different characters at different times. This structure keeps things intriguing and interesting for the audience.

	unjust things; and, to conclude, they are lying knaves.	215
DON PEDRO	First, I ask thee what they have done; thirdly, I ask thee what's their offence; sixth and lastly, why they are committed; and, to conclude, what you lay to their charge.	
CLAUDIO	Rightly reasoned, and in his own division, and, by my troth, there's one meaning well suited.	220
DON PEDRO	Who have you offended, masters, that you are thus bound to your answer? This learned constable is too cunning to be understood. What's your offence?	225
BORACHIO	Sweet Prince, let me go no farther to mine answer, do you hear me, and let this count kill me. I have deceived even your very eyes. What your wisdoms could not discover, these shallow fools have brought to light, who in the night overheard me confessing to this man how Don John your brother incensed me to slander the Lady Hero, how you were brought into the orchard and saw me court Margaret in Hero's garments, how you disgraced her, when you should marry her. My villainy they have upon record, which I had rather seal with my death than repeat over to my shame. The lady is dead upon mine and my master's false accusation, and, briefly, I desire nothing but the reward of a villain.	230 235 240
DON PEDRO	Runs not this speech like iron through your blood?	
CLAUDIO	I have drunk poison whiles he uttered it.	
DON PEDRO	But did my brother set thee on to this?	
BORACHIO	Yea, and paid me richly for the practice of it.	245
DON PEDRO	He is composed and framed of treachery, And fled he is upon this villainy.	
CLAUDIO	Sweet Hero! Now thy image doth appear In the rare semblance that I loved it first.	
DOGBERRY	Come, bring away the plaintiffs. By this time our sexton hath reformed Signior Leonato of the matter. And, masters, do not forget to specify, when time and place shall serve, that I am an ass.	250
VERGES	Here, here comes master Signior Leonato, and the Sexton too.	255

Re-enter LEONATO *and* ANTONIO *with the* SEXTON

LEONATO	Which is the villain? Let me see his eyes, That, when I note another man like him, I may avoid him. Which of these is he?	
BORACHIO	If you would know your wronger, look on me.	
LEONATO	Art thou the slave that with thy breath hast killed	260

Act 5, Scene 1

Mine innocent child?

BORACHIO   Yea, even I alone.

LEONATO No, not so, villain — thou beliest thyself.
Here stand a pair of honourable men,
A third is fled, that had a hand in it.
I thank you, princes, for my daughter's death.   265
Record it with your high and worthy deeds.
'Twas bravely done, if you bethink you of it.

CLAUDIO I know not how to pray your patience,
Yet I must speak. Choose your revenge yourself;
Impose me to what penance your invention   270
Can lay upon my sin. Yet sinned I not
But in mistaking.

DON PEDRO   By my soul, nor I;
And yet, to satisfy this good old man,
I would bend under any heavy weight
That he'll enjoin me to.   275

LEONATO I cannot bid you bid my daughter live —
That were impossible — but, I pray you both,
Possess the people in Messina here
How innocent she died, and if your love
Can labour ought in sad invention,   280
Hang her an epitaph upon her tomb
And sing it to her bones, sing it to-night.
Tomorrow morning come you to my house,
And since you could not be my son-in-law,
Be yet my nephew. My brother hath a daughter,   285
Almost the copy of my child that's dead,
And she alone is heir to both of us.
Give her the right you should have given her
cousin,
And so dies my revenge.

CLAUDIO   O noble sir,
Your over-kindness doth wring tears from me!   290
I do embrace your offer; and dispose
For henceforth of poor Claudio.

LEONATO Tomorrow then I will expect your coming;
Tonight I take my leave. This naughty man
Shall face to face be brought to Margaret,   295
Who I believe was packed in all this wrong,
Hired to it by your brother.

BORACHIO   No, by my soul, she was not,
Nor knew not what she did when she spoke to me,
But always hath been just and virtuous
In anything that I do know by her.   300

DOGBERRY Moreover, sir, which indeed is not under white and
black, this plaintiff here, the offender, did call me
ass. I beseech you, let it be remembered in his
punishment. And also, the Watch heard them talk
of one Deformed. They say he wears a key in his   305

---

263 He's sarcastically talking about Claudio and Don Pedro.

268-272 'I don't know how to ask you to hear me out, but I must speak. Choose your revenge yourself — force me to take whatever punishment you can come up with for my sin. But all I did wrong was make a mistake.'

275 'enjoin me to' means 'lay upon me'.

Shakespeare's Techniques

There is dramatic irony here — the audience knows that Hero is still alive and they expect this will be revealed now she's been proved innocent.

278-279 'Tell the people of Messina that she died innocent'.

279-280 'if your love can do this'.

281 An epitaph is something written in memory of someone who's died.

Theme — Deception and Misunderstanding

Leonato tells Claudio he must marry Hero's "cousin" to earn forgiveness. This deception will reunite Claudio and Hero.

291-292 'I welcome your offer, and poor Claudio is at your service for evermore.'

301-302 'under white and black' means 'written down'.

Act Five

Act 5, Scene 1

ear and a lock hanging by it, and borrows money in God's name, the which he hath used so long and never paid that now men grow hard-hearted and will lend nothing for God's sake — pray you, examine him upon that point. 310

LEONATO I thank thee for thy care and honest pains.

DOGBERRY Your worship speaks like a most thankful and reverend youth, and I praise God for you.

LEONATO There's for thy pains.

DOGBERRY God save the foundation! 315

LEONATO Go, I discharge thee of thy prisoner, and I thank thee.

DOGBERRY I leave an arrant knave with your worship, which I beseech your worship to correct yourself, for the example of others. God keep your worship! 320 I wish your worship well! God restore you to health! I humbly give you leave to depart, and if a merry meeting may be wished, God prohibit it! Come, neighbour.

Exeunt DOGBERRY *and* VERGES

LEONATO Until tomorrow morning, lords, farewell. 325

ANTONIO Farewell, my lords. We look for you tomorrow.

DON PEDRO We will not fail.

CLAUDIO Tonight I'll mourn with Hero.

LEONATO *(To the Watch)* Bring you these fellows on.
We'll talk with Margaret,
How her acquaintance grew with this lewd fellow.

Exeunt

---

314 Leonato gives Dogberry some money for his work.

315 'God save the foundation' was what people would say when they got a handout from a charitable organisation.

Shakespeare's Techniques

There is lots of <u>repetition</u> in Dogberry's language, which makes it more <u>confusing</u> and <u>humorous</u>.

Theme — Honour and Reputation

- Act 5, Scene 1 shows how important <u>honour</u> is to the characters. <u>Duels</u> were used to <u>defend</u> and <u>restore</u> honour — Leonato and Benedick both <u>challenge</u> Claudio in order to defend Hero. Fighting a duel showed that you were willing to <u>die</u> to <u>protect</u> your <u>reputation</u> — it was seen as <u>cowardly</u> and <u>dishonourable</u> to refuse a duel.

- Hero <u>doesn't appear</u> in this scene, even though most of it is <u>about her</u> and her <u>damaged reputation</u>. She is <u>powerless</u> to defend herself — she has to <u>play dead</u> until her <u>honour</u> is <u>restored</u> rather than live with the <u>shame</u>.

© Sam Goldwyn / Renaissance / BBC / Kobal / REX / Shutterstock

Act 5, Scene 2 — Benedick Writes a Poem

Benedick tries to write a <u>love poem</u> for Beatrice, but quickly <u>gives up</u>. He and Beatrice <u>bicker</u> and <u>tease</u> each other affectionately.

ACT 5, SCENE 2

© AF archive / Alamy Stock Photo

LEONATO'S GARDEN

Enter BENEDICK *and* MARGARET, *meeting*

BENEDICK	Pray thee, sweet Mistress Margaret, deserve well at my hands by helping me to the speech of Beatrice.
MARGARET	Will you then write me a sonnet in praise of my beauty? 5
BENEDICK	In so high a style, Margaret, that no man living shall come over it, for, in most comely truth, thou deservest it.
MARGARET	To have no man come over me! Why, shall I always keep below stairs? 10
BENEDICK	Thy wit is as quick as the greyhound's mouth — it catches.
MARGARET	And yours as blunt as the fencer's foils, which hit, but hurt not.
BENEDICK	A most manly wit, Margaret — it will not hurt a 15 woman. And so, I pray thee, call Beatrice. I give thee the bucklers.
MARGARET	Give us the swords; we have bucklers of our own.
BENEDICK	If you use them, Margaret, you must put in the pikes with a vice, and they are dangerous 20 weapons for maids.
MARGARET	Well, I will call Beatrice to you, who I think hath legs.

Exit MARGARET

BENEDICK	And therefore will come.

             (Sings) *The god of love,*   25
                  That sits above,
                  And knows me, and knows me,
                  How pitiful I deserve —
I mean in singing — but in loving, Leander the good swimmer, Troilus the first employer of   30 panders, and a whole bookful of these quondam carpet-mongers, whose names yet run smoothly in the even road of a blank verse, why, they were never so truly turned over and over as my poor self in love. Marry, I cannot show it in rhyme. I   35 have tried. I can find out no rhyme to 'lady' but 'baby', an innocent rhyme; for 'scorn', 'horn', a hard rhyme; for 'school', 'fool', a babbling rhyme; very ominous endings. No, I was not born under a rhyming planet, nor I cannot woo in festival   40 terms.

1-3 'do me a favour and help me write a poem for Beatrice.'

4 A 'sonnet' is a type of poem with fourteen lines, often about love.

6-8 'Margaret, it'll be in such a fine style that no living man will outdo it, because, truly, you're worth it.'

Theme — Love and Marriage

Margaret makes a <u>sexual joke</u> out of Benedick's words. This contrasts with writing the <u>sonnet</u>, which represents <u>courtly love</u>.

9-10 'What, will I always be a servant?'

13 'fencer's foils' are blunt swords used for practice.

16-17 'I give in — have the shields.' 'bucklers' were small round shields.

29 In Greek mythology, Leander drowned swimming across the sea to see Hero, the woman he loved.

30 Also in Greek mythology, Troilus was a Trojan who fell in love with Cressida.

31 'panders' refers to Cressida's uncle, Pandarus, who helped Troilus visit her.

31-32 'quondam carpet-mongers' are men who often visited women's bedrooms (which were carpeted).

Character — Benedick

Benedick knows that he <u>isn't</u> a <u>conventional courtly lover</u> — he isn't a good <u>poet</u> and can't <u>woo</u> in the <u>traditional</u> way.

Act 5, Scene 2

Character — Benedick

At the start of the play, Benedick hated the idea of love and marriage. Now he speaks openly about being in love and seems confident in his feelings.

52 'noisome' means 'smelly'.

54-55 'Your wit is so powerful, you've frightened the word out of its true meaning.'

57 'subscribe' means 'declare'.

60-62 'For all your parts as a whole, which add up to such a state of evil that they leave no space for any good part to be mixed in.'

Theme — Love and Marriage

Benedick and Beatrice still bicker and tease each other, but now it's a sign of love rather than hostility. Their bickering shows they have a more equal relationship than Claudio and Hero.

70 'Your words mean we can't be wise.'

72-76 'That's an example from the old days, Beatrice, when people were kinder to each other. Now, if a man doesn't build his own tomb before he dies, he'll be forgotten as soon as his funeral is over.'

78-82 'You may well ask: an hour of loud weeping, and a quarter of an hour of sniffling. So it's most sensible for a wise person, if his conscience lets him, to advertise his own good points, like I do.'

	Enter BEATRICE	
	Sweet Beatrice, wouldst thou come when I called thee?	
BEATRICE	Yea, signior, and depart when you bid me.	
BENEDICK	O, stay but till then!	45
BEATRICE	'Then' is spoken — fare you well now, and yet, ere I go, let me go with that I came, which is, with knowing what hath passed between you and Claudio.	
BENEDICK	Only foul words; and thereupon I will kiss thee.	50
BEATRICE	Foul words is but foul wind, and foul wind is but foul breath, and foul breath is noisome — therefore I will depart unkissed.	
BENEDICK	Thou hast frighted the word out of his right sense, so forcible is thy wit. But I must tell thee plainly, Claudio undergoes my challenge, and either I must shortly hear from him, or I will subscribe him a coward. And, I pray thee now, tell me for which of my bad parts didst thou first fall in love with me?	55
BEATRICE	For them all together, which maintained so politic a state of evil that they will not admit any good part to intermingle with them. But for which of my good parts did you first suffer love for me?	60
BENEDICK	Suffer love! A good epithet! I do suffer love indeed, for I love thee against my will.	65
BEATRICE	In spite of your heart, I think. Alas, poor heart! If you spite it for my sake, I will spite it for yours, for I will never love that which my friend hates.	
BENEDICK	Thou and I are too wise to woo peaceably.	
BEATRICE	It appears not in this confession. There's not one wise man among twenty that will praise himself.	70
BENEDICK	An old, an old instance, Beatrice, that lived in the time of good neighbours. If a man do not erect in this age his own tomb ere he dies, he shall live no longer in monument than the bell rings and the widow weeps.	75
BEATRICE	And how long is that, think you?	
BENEDICK	Question: why, an hour in clamour and a quarter in rheum. Therefore is it most expedient for the wise, if Don Worm, his conscience, find no impediment to the contrary, to be the trumpet of his own virtues, as I am to myself. So much for praising myself, who, I myself will bear witness, is praiseworthy: and now tell me, how doth your cousin?	80
		85
BEATRICE	Very ill.	
BENEDICK	And how do you?	
BEATRICE	Very ill too.	

Act 5, Scene 3 — Claudio Mourns at Hero's Tomb

BENEDICK	Serve God, love me and mend. There will I leave you too, for here comes one in haste.	90

Enter URSULA

URSULA	Madam, you must come to your uncle. Yonder's old coil at home. It is proved my Lady Hero hath been falsely accused, the Prince and Claudio mightily abused, and Don John is the author of all, who is fled and gone. Will you come presently?	95
BEATRICE	Will you go hear this news, signior?	
BENEDICK	I will live in thy heart, die in thy lap, and be buried in thy eyes; and moreover I will go with thee to thy uncle's.	

Exeunt

91-92 'There's a huge racket going on in the house.'

Shakespeare's Techniques

Shakespeare <u>sends</u> Ursula to tell them about <u>Don John's plot</u>. This <u>relieves</u> the <u>tension</u> — Benedick <u>won't</u> have to <u>duel</u> Claudio, and he and Beatrice can be <u>together</u>.

© Donald Cooper / photostage

Claudio and Don Pedro <u>mourn</u> at what they think is Hero's <u>tomb</u>. Then they set off for Claudio's <u>wedding</u> to Hero's '<u>cousin</u>'.

ACT 5, SCENE 3

A CHURCH

Enter DON PEDRO, CLAUDIO *and three or four with* tapers

CLAUDIO	Is this the monument of Leonato?	
LORD	It is, my lord.	
CLAUDIO	*(Reading out of a scroll)*	
	Done to death by slanderous tongues	
	Was the Hero that here lies.	
	Death, in guerdon of her wrongs,	5
	Gives her fame which never dies.	
	So the life that died with shame	
	Lives in death with glorious fame.	
	(Hangs up the scroll)	
	Hang thou there upon the tomb,	
	Praising her when I am dumb.	10
	Now, music, sound, and sing your solemn hymn.	
BALTHASAR	*(Sings)* *Pardon, goddess of the night,*	
	Those that slew thy virgin knight;	
	For the which, with songs of woe,	
	Round about her tomb they go.	15
	Midnight, assist our moan,	
	Help us to sigh and groan	
	Heavily, heavily.	
	Graves, yawn and yield your dead,	
	Till death be uttered	20
	Heavily, heavily.	

Stagecraft

The <u>stage</u> is <u>lit</u> by <u>torches</u> — this tells the audience that it's <u>night</u> and helps create a <u>sombre mood</u> for the scene.

1 'Leonato's family tomb'.

5 'guerdon' means 'repayment' or 'compensation'.

Shakespeare's Techniques

This scene is written in <u>verse</u>, including some <u>rhyming couplets</u>. This makes the language <u>solemn</u> and <u>formal</u>.

Act 5, Scene 4 — Hero is Alive

23 'rite' means 'ceremony'.

25-27 'The wolves have finished hunting and you can see the dawn.'

26 Phoebus is another name for Apollo, the Greek god of the sun who drove a chariot across the sky.

29 'several' means 'separate'.

30 'weeds' means 'clothes'.

32-33 'Let Hymen (the Greek god of marriage) help us reach a better result than the one we've been grieving over.'

Shakespeare's Techniques

Act 5, Scene 3 wraps up the tragic elements of the play. This structure enables the happy ending in the next scene.

CLAUDIO	Now, unto thy bones good night! Yearly will I do this rite.
DON PEDRO	Good morrow, masters — put your torches out. The wolves have preyed, and look, the gentle day, 25 Before the wheels of Phoebus, round about Dapples the drowsy east with spots of grey. Thanks to you all, and leave us. Fare you well.
CLAUDIO	Good morrow, masters — each his several way.
DON PEDRO	Come, let us hence, and put on other weeds, 30 And then to Leonato's we will go.
CLAUDIO	And Hymen now with luckier issue speed's Than this for whom we rendered up this woe!

Exeunt

Claudio arrives to marry Hero's 'cousin'. He doesn't know it's Hero until she takes her mask off. Benedick proposes to Beatrice and both couples decide to get married straightaway. There's a happy ending with lots of music and dancing.

ACT 5, SCENE 4

A ROOM IN LEONATO'S HOUSE

Enter LEONATO, ANTONIO, BENEDICK, BEATRICE, MARGARET, URSULA, FRIAR FRANCIS *and* HERO

3 'Of the wrong-doing you heard us speak of.'

6 'In the course of our investigation.'

8-9 'Me too, otherwise I would have been bound by honour to fight young Claudio over it.'

Theme — Deception and Misunderstanding

The women put on masks so Claudio can't see Hero's face. This links back to the masked ball, when the men wore masks and Claudio and Hero got engaged.

17 'confirmed countenance' means 'serious expression'.

18 'I need to ask you a favour'.

FRIAR FRANCIS	Did I not tell you she was innocent?
LEONATO	So are the Prince and Claudio, who accused her Upon the error that you heard debated. But Margaret was in some fault for this, Although against her will, as it appears 5 In the true course of all the question.
ANTONIO	Well, I am glad that all things sort so well.
BENEDICK	And so am I, being else by faith enforced To call young Claudio to a reckoning for it.
LEONATO	Well, daughter, and you gentlewomen all, 10 Withdraw into a chamber by yourselves, And when I send for you, come hither masked.

Exeunt ladies

The Prince and Claudio promised by this hour
To visit me. You know your office, brother:
You must be father to your brother's daughter 15
And give her to young Claudio.

ANTONIO	Which I will do with confirmed countenance.
BENEDICK	Friar, I must entreat your pains, I think.

Act Five

Act 5, Scene 4

FRIAR FRANCIS	To do what, signior?
BENEDICK	To bind me, or undo me — one of them.
	Signior Leonato, truth it is, good signior,
	Your niece regards me with an eye of favour.
LEONATO	That eye my daughter lent her. 'Tis most true.
BENEDICK	And I do with an eye of love requite her.
LEONATO	The sight whereof I think you had from me,
	From Claudio and the Prince: but what's your will?
BENEDICK	Your answer, sir, is enigmatical,
	But, for my will, my will is your good will
	May stand with ours, this day to be conjoined
	In the state of honourable marriage,
	In which, good friar, I shall desire your help.
LEONATO	My heart is with your liking.
FRIAR FRANCIS	And my help.
	Here comes the Prince and Claudio.

Enter DON PEDRO *and* CLAUDIO *and two or three others*

DON PEDRO	Good morrow to this fair assembly.
LEONATO	Good morrow, Prince; good morrow, Claudio.
	We here attend you. Are you yet determined
	Today to marry with my brother's daughter?
CLAUDIO	I'll hold my mind, were she an Ethiope.
LEONATO	Call her forth, brother — here's the friar ready.

Exit ANTONIO

DON PEDRO	Good morrow, Benedick. Why, what's the matter,
	That you have such a February face,
	So full of frost, of storm and cloudiness?
CLAUDIO	I think he thinks upon the savage bull.
	Tush, fear not, man, we'll tip thy horns with gold
	And all Europa shall rejoice at thee,
	As once Europa did at lusty Jove,
	When he would play the noble beast in love.
BENEDICK	Bull Jove, sir, had an amiable low,
	And some such strange bull leaped your father's cow,
	And got a calf in that same noble feat
	Much like to you, for you have just his bleat.

Re-enter ANTONIO, *with the ladies masked*

CLAUDIO	For this I owe you. Here comes other reck'nings.
	Which is the lady I must seize upon?
ANTONIO	This same is she, and I do give you her.
CLAUDIO	Why, then she's mine. Sweet, let me see your face.
LEONATO	No, that you shall not, till you take her hand
	Before this friar and swear to marry her.
CLAUDIO	Give me your hand before this holy friar.
	I am your husband, if you like of me.

Line numbers: 20, 25, 30, 35, 40, 45, 50, 55

20 'To make me, or break me — one of the two.'

Theme — Deception and Misunderstanding
Leonato refers to the tricks that made Benedick and Beatrice fall in love, but Benedick doesn't understand the references.

27 'enigmatical' means 'mysterious'.
28-30 'I want to marry Beatrice and I hope you'll wish us well'.

38 'I'll do as I've promised, even if she's Ethiopian.' Ethiopia was a semi-mythical place for people in Elizabethan England — it's a bit like saying 'even if she's a Martian'. A modern audience would consider this comment racist.

Shakespeare's Techniques
Claudio uses cuckold jokes and classical imagery to tease Benedick. He says Benedick will be a successful lover like Jove, so shouldn't worry about his wife being unfaithful.

45-47 In Roman mythology, Jove, the king of the gods, turned himself into a bull to seduce a woman called Europa.

48-51 'When Jove was a bull, he had a lovely bellow, and it seems some bull mated with your father's cow, and produced a calf like you, because you bellow in just the same way.'

Act 5, Scene 4

HERO	*(Unmasking)* And when I lived, I was your other wife,	60
	And when you loved, you were my other husband.	
CLAUDIO	Another Hero!	
HERO	Nothing certainer.	
	One Hero died defiled, but I do live,	
	And surely as I live, I am a maid.	
DON PEDRO	The former Hero! Hero that is dead!	65
LEONATO	She died, my lord, but whiles her slander lived.	
FRIAR FRANCIS	All this amazement can I qualify,	
	When after that the holy rites are ended,	
	I'll tell you largely of fair Hero's death.	
	Meantime let wonder seem familiar,	70
	And to the chapel let us presently.	
BENEDICK	Soft and fair, friar. Which is Beatrice?	
BEATRICE	*(Unmasking)* I answer to that name. What is your will?	
BENEDICK	Do not you love me?	
BEATRICE	Why, no, no more than reason.	
BENEDICK	Why, then your uncle and the Prince and Claudio	75
	Have been deceived — they swore you did.	
BEATRICE	Do not you love me?	
BENEDICK	Troth, no, no more than reason.	
BEATRICE	Why, then my cousin, Margaret, and Ursula	
	Are much deceived, for they did swear you did.	
BENEDICK	They swore that you were almost sick for me.	80
BEATRICE	They swore that you were well-nigh dead for me.	
BENEDICK	'Tis no such matter. Then you do not love me?	
BEATRICE	No, truly, but in friendly recompense.	
LEONATO	Come, cousin, I am sure you love the gentleman.	
CLAUDIO	And I'll be sworn upon't that he loves her,	85
	For here's a paper written in his hand,	
	A halting sonnet of his own pure brain,	
	Fashioned to Beatrice.	
HERO	And here's another	
	Writ in my cousin's hand, stolen from her pocket,	
	Containing her affection unto Benedick.	90
BENEDICK	A miracle! Here's our own hands against our hearts. Come, I will have thee, but, by this light, I take thee for pity.	
BEATRICE	I would not deny you, but, by this good day, I yield upon great persuasion, and partly to save your life, for I was told you were in a consumption.	95
BENEDICK	Peace! I will stop your mouth. *(Kisses her)*	
DON PEDRO	How dost thou, Benedick, the married man?	
BENEDICK	I'll tell thee what, Prince; a college of wit-crackers cannot flout me out of my humour. Dost thou	100

63 'defiled' means 'disgraced'.

Shakespeare's Techniques

The plan is explained using imagery of life and death — Hero could only 'live' again once her good reputation was restored.

67-71 'I'll answer all your questions after the service, when I'll give you all the details of lovely Hero's death. In the meantime, just take it all for granted and let's go into the chapel.'

Shakespeare's Techniques

Benedick and Beatrice say almost the same thing — Shakespeare uses repetition to reflect how the tricking scenes mirror each other.

81 'well-nigh' means 'just about'.

83 'Only as a friend.'

87 'halting' means 'clumsy'.

Theme — Love and Marriage

Even though they aren't conventional lovers, Benedick and Beatrice wrote love poems for each other — as courtly lovers would do. These poems are used as proof of their love.

92-93 'Come on, I'll marry you, but only because I feel sorry for you.'

94-96 'I won't turn you down, but I swear I'm only giving in after some serious persuasion, and partly to save your life, because I was told you were wasting away.'

99-100 'a college of jokers couldn't taunt me out of my good mood.'

Act 5, Scene 4

think I care for a satire or an epigram? No. If a man will be beaten with brains, a' shall wear nothing handsome about him. In brief, since I do purpose to marry, I will think nothing to any purpose that the world can say against it, and therefore never flout at me for what I have said against it, for man is a giddy thing, and this is my conclusion. For thy part, Claudio, I did think to have beaten thee, but in that thou art like to be my kinsman, live unbruised and love my cousin. 110

CLAUDIO   I had well hoped thou wouldst have denied Beatrice, that I might have cudgelled thee out of thy single life, to make thee a double-dealer, which, out of question, thou wilt be, if my cousin do not look exceeding narrowly to thee. 115

BENEDICK   Come, come, we are friends. Let's have a dance ere we are married, that we may lighten our own hearts and our wives' heels.

LEONATO   We'll have dancing afterward.

BENEDICK   First, of my word! Therefore play, music. Prince, 120 thou art sad. Get thee a wife, get thee a wife! There is no staff more reverend than one tipped with horn.

Enter a Messenger

MESSENGER   My lord, your brother John is ta'en in flight, And brought with armed men back to Messina. 125

BENEDICK   Think not on him till tomorrow. I'll devise thee brave punishments for him. Strike up, pipers.

Dance

Exeunt

105

100-101 A 'satire' and an 'epigram' are both witty poems. Benedick is saying he doesn't care if people use their wit to insult him.

103-108 'since I plan to get married, I won't listen to criticism, so don't tease me for what I've said about marriage in the past, because men do change their minds, and that's all there is to it.'

112 'cudgelled' means 'beaten'.

113 Here, 'double-dealer' can mean 'adulterer' (in the sense of cheating) or 'married man' (the opposite of being single).

114-115 'which you certainly will be unless Beatrice keeps a close eye on you.'

Character — Benedick

In Act 1, Scene 1, Benedick didn't want Claudio to "turn husband". Now he's getting married and is encouraging Don Pedro to do the same.

122-123 'There's no better walking stick than one with a horn handle.'

Shakespeare's Techniques

Music and dancing reflect the feeling of celebration and symbolise the play's happy ending.

Theme — Love and Marriage

Shakespeare presents the two relationships in antithesis (as opposites). The couples have different approaches to love, but both end in marriage.

- Initially, Benedick and Beatrice insult each other and mock marriage. After the tricks, their conversations become more personal and they finally admit their true feelings for each other. Their marriage shows how much they have grown and changed as characters.

- Claudio falls in love with Hero in Act 1, Scene 1, but this is based on her beauty and reputation rather than her personality. His opinion of her changes quickly when he thinks she's been unfaithful and when she's proved innocent — his feelings seem artificial. Their marriage represents Claudio being forgiven and Hero's reputation being restored.

© Sam Goldwyn / Renaissance / BBC / Kobal / REX / Shutterstock

Act Five — Practice Questions

Quick Questions

1) What does Antonio want to do to defend his family's honour?

2) How does Claudio react when Benedick challenges him to a duel?

3) Who explains Don John's plan to Don Pedro and Claudio?

4) What three things does Claudio have to do to earn Leonato's forgiveness?

5) In Act 5, Scene 2, what does Benedick struggle to write?

6) Who tells Benedick and Beatrice about Don John's plan being uncovered?

7) Why do the women put on masks in Act 5, Scene 4?

8) How do Claudio and Hero prove that Benedick and Beatrice love each other?

9) Who tells Don Pedro that he should get married?

10) What happens to Don John at the end of the play?

In-depth Questions

1) In Act 5, Scene 1, how does Shakespeare make it sound as though Leonato is grieving?

2) How does Shakespeare create tension in Act 5, Scene 1?

3) Explain whether you think Borachio is actually sorry for taking part in Don John's plot.

4) Compare how Benedick is presented in Act 5 with how he is presented earlier in the play.

5) Do you feel sorry for Claudio and Don Pedro in Act 5? Why / why not?

6) Describe the role that deception plays in Act 5.

7) How do you think a modern audience might respond to the play's ending?
   Do you think they would respond differently from Shakespeare's audience?

8) Imagine you are directing a production of the play. You want to make the atmosphere
   in Act 5, Scene 3 as sad and sombre as possible. Write some instructions for the cast
   and crew, describing how you want the scene to look and how it should be acted.

Practice Questions

Quick Questions

1) Find a scene where the mood is tragic.

2) Find a line that shows Benedick's mistrust of women.

3) Describe a moment in the play where Shakespeare uses language to create humour.

4) Find an example of a rhyming couplet.

5) Give three words that describe Claudio's personality.

6) Describe part of a scene where the mood is light-hearted.

7) Find a scene that contains dramatic irony.

8) "Give not this rotten orange to your friend" is an example of what type of imagery?

9) Describe a time when Don John acts deceitfully.

Theme Questions

1) How does Shakespeare present courtly love in the play?

2) Describe how Beatrice is presented as an unconventional Elizabethan woman.

3) How does honour affect Leonato's actions during the play?

4) Find a scene where social status is important and explain the impact it has on the scene.

5) Compare Benedick and Claudio's attitudes to marriage.

6) Find an example of a misunderstanding in the play and explain its significance to the plot.

7) Who do you think is the most loyal character in the play? Explain your answer.

8) How do the male characters view and treat women in the play?

9) How does deception lead to the play's happy ending?

Practice Questions

Character Questions

1) Explain how Shakespeare presents Claudio as suspicious.

2) Do you think that Don Pedro is an honourable character? Why / why not?

3) Describe how Beatrice changes over the course of the play.

4) Explain the role of Margaret in the play.

5) How does Shakespeare present Friar Francis as a sensible character?

6) Do you think that Hero is a weak character? Explain your answer.

7) Explain how Shakespeare shows the different sides to Leonato's character.

8) How does Shakespeare present Don John as an ineffective villain?

9) Do you think that Benedick has changed completely by the end of the play? Why / why not?

Technique Questions

1) What is the significance of hunting imagery in the play?

2) How does Shakespeare use dramatic irony to create humour when Benedick is tricked?

3) Why do you think that Claudio often speaks in verse?

4) Why does Shakespeare use lots of puns and wordplay in *Much Ado About Nothing*?

5) Choose a soliloquy in the play and explain its effect.

6) How are songs and music used in the play?

7) How does the setting of Messina create a peaceful atmosphere?

8) In what ways is *Much Ado About Nothing* a typical Shakespearean comedy?

9) Find an example of a contrast in the play and explain the effect it has.

The Characters in 'Much Ado About Nothing'

Phew! You should be an expert on *Much Ado About Nothing* by now. But if you want a bit of light relief and a quick recap of what happens in the play, read through *Much Ado About Nothing — The Cartoon*...

Benedick

Beatrice

Hero

Claudio

Don Pedro

Leonato

Don John

Friar Francis

Dogberry

Borachio

Conrade

William Shakespeare's 'Much Ado About Nothing'

EPMA43